SAVE YOURSELVES!

ONE FAMILY'S STORY OF HOLOCAUST SURVIVAL

RONALD J. BERGER

LITTLE CREEK PRESS®
AND BOOK DESIGN
Mineral Point, Wisconsin USA

Little Creek Press® and Book Design
A Division of Kristin Mitchell Design, Inc.
5341 Sunny Ridge Road
Mineral Point, Wisconsin 53565

Book Design and Project Coordination:
Little Creek Press

First Edition
January 2018

Printed in Wisconsin, United States of America

For more information or to order books:
visit www.littlecreekpress.com

Library of Congress Control Number: 2017962222

ISBN-13: 978-1-942586-29-6
ISBN-10: 1-942586-29-9

◆ ◆ ◆

Dedicated to my beloved father and mother,

Michael and Mildred Berger,

and my beloved uncle and aunt,

Sol and Gertrude (Gusta) Berger

◆ ◆ ◆

CONTENTS

Prologue

This book tells the story of my father's and uncle's survival of the Holocaust in Nazi-occupied Poland during World War II. They were among the 10 percent of Polish Jewry who survived the war. My father, Michael Berger (1921-1994), endured several concentration camps, including the infamous camp at Auschwitz, as well as a horrific winter death march. My uncle, Sol Berger (1919-2016), survived outside of the camps by passing as a Catholic among anti-Semitic Poles, including a group of anti-Nazi Polish partisans, eventually becoming an officer in the Soviet Army.

My family's story, some may be surprised to learn, is one that I did not hear in any detail until 1988, when I was 37 years old. But ever since then, it has been a story I keep coming back to, because for me it is the greatest story ever told.

That my exposure to this story came rather late in my life is in many ways unsurprising, because in the immediate postwar years, the Holocaust as we have come to know it was not understood as such. Although the discovery of the concentration camps by U.S. infantrymen at the end of the war was well reported in the press, the atrocity of the camps was generally portrayed as part of the general horror of war; and the sight of dead bodies and emaciated camp survivors was viewed more with revulsion than compassion. Additionally, the term "Holocaust" did not become part of popular discourse about what had transpired until the late 1950s, and even then the particularity of Jewish victimization that befell my Polish relatives and others like them was rather opaque.[1]

Jewish victimization was certainly acknowledged at the Nuremberg trials of Nazi criminals that the Allies conducted after the war, but it was subsumed under the broader categories of "war crimes" and "crimes against humanity" and soon half forgotten. The word "Jew" was not even mentioned in Alain Resnais's otherwise brilliant 1955 documentary film *Night and Fog*. William Shirer's *The Rise and Fall of the Third Reich*, a 1960 bestseller, devoted just two to three percent of its some 1,200 pages to the Jewish genocide. And even works that have now become classics, such as Elie Wiesel's *Night* (published in 1960) and Ann Frank's diary (published in Dutch in 1947 and English in 1952), had inauspicious beginnings.[2]

In 1946, when my father first arrived in the United States, no one, not even our Jewish relatives, was particularly interested in hearing about his ordeal. People would say things like, "We suffered too. Did you know we couldn't get sugar [during the war] and that gasoline was rationed?" So my father and other survivors like him stopped talking about their experiences. At that time the idea of the Holocaust "survivor" who was highly respected as a witness to history had yet to become a cultural phenomenon. The world was not ready to listen to their stories, to say nothing of embracing them as wise and revered figures. They were viewed as "displaced persons," "refugees," "greenhorns."

A key turning point in this unfortunate view of survivors was the 1961 trial of Adolf Eichmann. Eichmann, a key architect of the genocide of European Jews that the Nazis called the Final Solution, had been apprehended by Israeli agents in Argentina and taken to Israel for criminal prosecution. The trial, which was publicized around the world, was the first time large numbers of survivors began telling their stories in public. Gradually, more and more survivors found sympathetic listeners to their stories, but this changing culture had not yet filtered down to me.

At that time, too, I was completely unaware of another cultural phenomenon that was emerging: the notion of the second generation of children of survivors, a group that first gained national recognition in the late 1970s, especially through the publication of Helen Epstein's book, *Children of the Holocaust: Conversations with Sons and Daughters of Survivors*, in 1979.

This second-generation movement was part of a general cultural interest in family roots and genealogy that emerged in the United States in the 1970s, an interest that gained momentum after the 1977 broadcast of the television miniseries *Roots*, based on Alex Haley's epic novel about a fictional African-American family. *Roots* was followed the next year by the broadcast of *Holocaust*, a television miniseries about two fictional families, one Jewish and one German, which was viewed by some 120 million people in the United States alone. Historically comprehensive in scope, *Holocaust* was in many ways a mini-survey course on the Holocaust, and it was my first detailed exposure to what had transpired. Still, I had little knowledge of my own family's story and did not yet think of myself as part of the second generation.

◆ ◆ ◆

I was born in Los Angeles, California, in 1951. When I was 6 or 7 years old, my father later reminded me, I asked him why I only

Children, Save Yourselves!

had grandparents (who had immigrated to the United States before World War II) on my mother's side of the family, while all my friends had two sets of grandparents. At that time all he said was that they had died. When I was a little older, he did tell me about being in a concentration camp and about his agony over losing his parents. At a young age, however, I do not think I really understood what being in a concentration camp entailed. Back then, it seemed to me, the only observable trace of his ordeal was the blue number 160914 tattooed on his left arm. Moreover, I cannot recall any attention given to the subject during all my years in public school or later even in college at the University of California, Los Angeles. Nor can I recall it mentioned in Hebrew school during the period of my life when I was preparing for my bar mitzvah. Quite frankly, my most vivid images of World War II came not from the Holocaust but from movies about the experiences and heroics of American soldiers.

I was raised in a working- and middle-class Jewish enclave on the west side of Los Angeles. Until I was 8 years old, we lived next door to the family of one of my father's friends, a man who also was a Holocaust survivor. Richard Stewart had been in one of the same concentration camps as my father, Auschwitz-Monowitz, the Auschwitz subsidiary that provided slave labor for I.G. Farben, a German petrochemical corporation. There were other survivors (as well as prewar European immigrants) in our social network and extended family. I did not, however, realize any of this at the time. I was surrounded by people with European accents, which seemed completely natural to me, and I had no idea of the implications of all this.

The public schools I attended in Los Angeles had large Jewish populations. It was not uncommon for classrooms to be virtually empty on the Jewish holidays of Rosh Hashanah and Yom Kippur. At Christmastime I did not feel left out or envious of Christian children because we thought that the practice of receiving gifts over an eight-day period for Hanukkah was much better than a one-day holiday. Only later did I discover that many Christian children in the United States enjoy a veritable orgy of gifts on that one day—a sign of American affluence—that far surpasses anything we received during our week-long celebration.

My parents' religious beliefs could best be described as agnostic, although they always self-identified as Jews and held strong nationalist sentiments toward Israel. For us, being Jewish was more of an ethnic-cultural identity than a theological faith. During my childhood, we did observe all of the major Jewish holidays, and it was assumed that at 13 years of age I would have my bar mitzvah, which I did. But further Jewish education was not obligatory, although I did study Hebrew for another six months. Because I was raised in a liberal Jewish milieu, I felt as though I were an assimilated American. And this was fine with me. I did not believe that being Jewish made me an outsider until I moved to southeastern Wisconsin in 1981 upon accepting a teaching position at the University of Wisconsin-Whitewater.

UW-Whitewater is located in a small college town between Madison and Milwaukee, about two hours by car from Chicago. In Whitewater and the neighboring small towns in which I lived for several years, there are few, if any, Jews. Most of the people in these communities are either Catholics or Lutherans who have little contact with people from non-Christian backgrounds. Within a month or two after I first arrived, I was invited to dinner at a faculty member's house. After dinner the conversation somehow turned to religion, and our hostess said, in what seemed like a non sequitur, "Those Jews have a lot of nerve thinking they are the chosen people!" Then there was the little 7-year-old, a neighbor of mine, who expressed confusion to her parents when she found out I was Jewish because she thought that all "Jews had horns." Several years later, a 12-year-old friend of my stepson casually remarked, "Jews are bad people."

At other times I heard comments pertaining to people who would "Jew you down." The first time I heard this was from our elderly departmental secretary. She spoke with no vehemence, as though the idiom were not steeped in prejudice. A few years later, after I married into an extended family of Wisconsin Synod Lutherans, my father-in-law made the "Jew you down" remark. I thought of saying something to him but decided to let the matter rest.

There also was the time I was in a liquor store buying a bottle of wine or some beer, when the salesclerk told an anti-Semitic joke to the customer he seemed to know who was standing next to me. I do not even remember the specifics of the joke; it was something about a Jewish businessman who committed arson insurance fraud and moved to Florida. The clerk, of course, did not know I would find the joke objectionable, but again I said nothing. This particular battle I did not need to fight. But I did feel as though I were invisible.

It is not that I am complaining about all this. These little affronts to my ethnic ancestry pale in comparison to the real thing. However, they are part of the life trajectory that was leading to my encounter with my family's story of the Holocaust.

My own interest in exploring my father's past, however, was piqued at a lecture I attended at the university in 1987. Robert Clary, the actor most known for his role as Louis LeBeau in the television comedy series *Hogan's Heroes*, spoke to a standing-room-only audience of more than 800 people. The TV show was still rather popular, and I had never seen so many people turn out for a non-sporting event at the university. Clary's topic was the Holocaust and his survival of it. He explained that for most of his postwar life he had kept still about his experience to avoid the painful remembering of his "31 months of hell." But as he turned 60, he said, he began to realize that soon there would no longer exist living testimony to the Holocaust. Clary added that he was particularly concerned about the problem of Holocaust deniers who, in spite of all the evidence to the contrary, continue to dispute that the atrocities occurred.

During the audience question-and-answer period that followed Clary's speech, a young woman stood up, said she was 25 years old, and said she was outraged that she had not been taught about or "heard of the Holocaust" before Clary's lecture. The audience, including myself, was taken aback by her comment. However, what also soon struck me was how little I knew about the Holocaust, and in particular about what had happened to my father and his family. This led to an immediate phone call back home. "We have to record your story," I told my father. And he seemed pleased. He was ready for someone to ask, and happy that he would be able to, in his words, "leave a legacy for my family." Along the way, my uncle agreed to tell his story too.

◆ ◆ ◆

What began as a family genealogy project also evolved into a scholarly interest about the Holocaust. I began to educate myself about the subject and teach a university course, and I eventually published a number of scholarly articles and four books.[3] My first book about my family's story, which evaluated their experiences from a sociological perspective, was published in 1995. Although my father was able to read the final manuscript, he died shortly before it appeared in print.

My father was diagnosed with an aggressive form of lung cancer in November 1994 and died before the end of the year. But from 1988 to 1994 he spoke often in public about his wartime experiences—to students in various educational settings (from middle school to college) and as a docent at the Simon Wiesenthal Center's Museum of Tolerance in Los Angeles.

Children, Save Yourselves!

My uncle was initially reluctant to speak in public, in part because he felt he was not an authentic representative of the survivor experience because he had not been in a concentration camp. But when my father was dying of cancer, he asked my uncle to promise him two things: help my mother take care of her financial affairs, and take his place as our family's representative of the Holocaust. Hence my uncle also became a public speaker—for nearly 20 years. He also videotaped his story for both Steven Spielberg's Shoah Foundation and the Jewish Federation of Los Angeles; and he was one of the survivors who was featured in the audio production *Voices of the Shoah: Remembrances of the Holocaust*, which was broadcast on national radio in 2000.[4]

Over the years, my uncle made additional video recordings for our family—with the help of his daughter, Marlene, and son, Jack—about his experiences both during the war and after arriving in the United States. My uncle also introduced me to Dr. Alexander Bialywlos White, a survivor from his hometown who resided in Scottsdale, Arizona. I spoke with Alex and he sent me a copy of his self-published memoir that he wrote about his experience.[5] I drew on this additional material for my second book about my family that was published in 2011. Lastly, Jesse Morris, the son of Marlene and her husband Lee, became interested in learning more about his grandfather, as well as his grandmother Gertrude (also a survivor), and he helped them self-publish a book in 2013 that contained further details about his grandparents.[6]

All of my previous books were academic in nature, aimed at a scholarly audience, and published by academic presses. *Children, Save Yourselves!* is aimed at a lay audience and affords me an opportunity to tell my family's story as I wish to tell it, drawing on all the information I now have at my disposal, one last time.[7]

I

Krosno

Poland was the primary "killing field" of the Holocaust. With the largest Jewish population in Europe, more than half of the Jews who were killed were Polish Jews, and thousands of others from other countries were exterminated in death camps located there. Most of my extended European family was among those who were killed, but my father and uncle were among the 10 percent of Polish Jews who survived.

Jewish life in Poland can be traced to the tenth century, when Jews, often fleeing persecution, emigrated from the west, south, and east. The medieval kings and princes of Poland, who were eager to develop a mercantile middle class, often welcomed Jewish refugees, in spite of objections from the Roman Catholic Church, which prohibited Jewish residents in towns under its control. In various localities Jews were granted legal charters that gave them the right to practice their religion as well as engage in commercial trade and money-lending activities, which were especially open to Jews because of the Church's prohibition of usury. Nonetheless, Polish Jews suffered the anti-Semitic hostility and discriminatory treatment that was generally true of Jews throughout Europe.[1]

The circumstances of Polish Jews varied from one locality to another. They were often barred from occupational guilds and denied opportunities to own land. Mostly they pursued an economic livelihood as merchants, craftsmen, or professionals. Although some Jews engaged in agriculture, most lived in urban areas. In the fourteenth and fifteenth centuries, Jews played a significant role as middlemen in the trade between Poland and other European countries. Because of links with Jewish communities outside of Poland, Jewish merchants at times gained advantage over non-Jewish businessmen. In addition, Jews functioned in administrative capacities as estate managers for wealthy landowners and the nobility. At times these positions involved collecting taxes and supervising the labor of peasant sharecroppers. All this bred resentment among Poles, especially Ukrainian Poles, another ethnic minority group in Poland,[2] who saw Jews as their economic competitors and as the source of their misfortune. Along with the hostility engendered by the Church, such resentment often broke out in violent pogroms against the Jewish population.

By the latter part of the eighteenth century, Poland was divided among three conquering powers: Russia, Prussia, and Austria. Under these regimes Jews gained a measure of equality, provided they were willing to abandon their religious-cultural traditions and distinctiveness as a people and adopt the culture of the dominant society. According to historian Israel Gutman, the opportunity for assimilation "found a ready response among a limited sector of wealthy and educated Jews ... [who] played a role in the development of a capitalist economy in Poland, and ... [who] distinguished themselves in science ... and the arts, clearing a path for modern culture to penetrate into Jewish society." But as these Jews assimilated into the dominant culture, they were essentially "lost to the Jewish people within a generation or two, whereas the Jewish masses remained faithful to their heritage."[3]

By the early part of the twentieth century, Jews for the most part remained a non-assimilated community that stood out from the general Polish population by their dress, habits, names and surnames, and mannerisms. But even Jews who wanted to modernize were generally denied the opportunities to do so. It was essentially a caste system from which escape was difficult, and Polish Jews were among the poorest of all the Jewish communities in Europe. Still, leaders of the rising right-wing Polish nationalist movement began advocating a political program that rejected Jewish assimilation and that, on the eve of World War I, embarked on an aggressive anti-Semitic campaign that included economic boycotts of Jewish businesses. At the same time Zionism, the national liberation movement to create a Jewish state in Palestine (now Israel), also took hold among some Polish Jews.

Poland gained its sovereignty in the aftermath of World War I. This national rebirth, however, was accompanied by much internal political turmoil and anti-Jewish violence. The Versailles Minority Treaty, which the victors of World War I imposed on Poland, guaranteed political rights to minorities, including Jews and Ukrainians, who each constituted about 10 percent of the Polish population. The treaty was perceived by Poles as an insult to their national honor, and discrimination and violence against Jews, tolerated if not condoned by the government, became a means of defiance.

Poland experienced 14 separate governments between 1918 and 1925, until Marshal Józef Piłsudski seized power in a military coup in 1926. The Jews actually fared better under Piłsudski's regime, but after his death in 1935, the new government returned to anti-Semitic zealotry. Efforts were made to dislodge Jews from positions of influence and to close down opportunities for aspiring Jewish youths to be admitted to institutions of higher education. Jews continued to be the object of economic boycotts as well as anti-Semitic propaganda and violence. The Polish government even took a cue from its Nazi neighbor in Germany and began to advocate emigration of Jews (to Madagascar, for example) as a solution to the "problem" of Jews in their midst. In a 1937 speech to the Polish parliament, Foreign Minister Józef Beck argued that Poland had space for only about one-half million Jews. Such was the state of affairs for Polish Jews on the eve of World War II.

◆ ◆ ◆

My father, Michael, and my uncle, Sol, grew up against this historical backdrop. Their birthplace was the city of Krosno, which had a population of about 6,300 at the time of their birth, but grew to about 18,000 (with about 2,200-2,500 Jews) by the late 1930s. Krosno is located in the western Galacia region of southern Poland, about 170 kilometers southeast of Kraków. It was founded in the fourteenth century, and weaving played an important role in its economic development, perhaps contributing to the name of the city, which means "loom" in Polish. By the sixteenth century, Krosno had emerged as an important industrial, trade, and craft center and became known as "little Kraków."[4]

Jews first settled in Krosno in the fifteenth century, but the Catholic Church and its congregants opposed their presence, and there was no organized Jewish life to be found. But in the nineteenth century, when Galacia was annexed by Austria, Jews were granted equality under the law, and they began migrating to Krosno in greater numbers. My grandfather, Jacob Berger (1873-1942), a tailor by profession, moved to Krosno from the nearby town of Korczyna in the late 1800s and bought a home that doubled as a tailor shop and residence. A 1929 Krosno business directory listed 205 Jews, with Jacob as one of 24 tailors. The directory included Jews who worked in a range of occupations: blacksmithery, carpentry, construction, fabrics, haberdashery, photography, printing, jewelry, cookery, restaurants, butchering, dairying, dentistry, pharmacy, and medicine, among others. Krosno also had an oil refinery, a glass factory, and a shoe and rubber factory.

Jacob had two wives. With Miriam Fabian Rieger (1876-1908), his first wife, he had five daughters: Helena (1897-1938), Frances (1900-1985), Bertha (1902-1942), Eleanor (1904-1987), and Rose (1906-2003). After Miriam died while giving birth to Rose, Jacob married Miriam's younger sister, Rosa (1893-1942), as was the Jewish custom at that time. Rosa gave birth to four sons: Moses (1913-1943), Joshua (1916-1943), Solomon (1919-2016), and Michael (1921-1994).[5] Because they were the youngest, Solomon and Michael had a closer relationship with each other than they did with their other siblings.[6]

Economic opportunities for Jews were limited in Poland, and the Berger children, like many other European Jews, wanted to seek a better life in the United States, which European Jews referred to as the *Goldene Medina*, or Golden State.[7] Jacob and Rosa never considered leaving themselves; their lives were settled and they considered Poland their homeland. But they did not discourage their children from seeking the American dream. Frances and Eleanor were the first to immigrate in 1920, first to Chicago and later to Los Angeles, before Michael was even born.

Rather than immigrating to America, Helena and Rose went to Berlin, Germany, when Michael and Sol were still young children. The day after the Kristallnacht pogrom of November 9-10, 1938, the infamous attack by Nazi troops against German Jews, Rose went to the hospital where Helena was supposed to be having surgery.[8] When Rose arrived, the hospital staff told her that Helena had died, for reasons that were unexplained.

Fearing the threat of Nazism, Rose and her husband, Jack Landerer, had applied for U.S. visas. Helena and her husband, Sigmund Gebel, also had applied for themselves and their two teenage children, Arnold and Marion. Just prior to the outbreak of World War II, which began on September 1, 1939, the papers they needed to immigrate to the United States were approved. The five of them sailed from Bremerhaven aboard a German freight ship; and while traveling on the ship, Rose gave birth to her son Sheldon. The journey took six weeks as the ship headed south through the Panama Canal and then north to Los Angeles.

When Michael and Sol became older, they wanted to follow their sisters to America. They applied for U.S. visas, which were registered with the U.S. Consulate in Warsaw, and expected to receive approval to immigrate in 1941. Unfortunately, the war stopped all immigration. They are the only two relatives from our immediate Polish family who had not emigrated before the war to survive.

Jacob was a kind, hard-working, and religiously observant man. Every morning he went to synagogue to pray, came home and had breakfast, and then worked the rest of the day. He worked every day but the Sabbath, which began at sundown on Friday evening. When he returned from Friday services, he usually brought home three or four indigent Jews for a Sabbath meal.

Rosa, in turn, took care of the home and prepared the meals. The traditional chicken in a pot, gefilte fish, challah, and chicken or parsley soup were favorite meals. The kitchen was her domain, although she had a maid to help her. And there were a lot of people to feed, because Jacob employed a group of tailors who worked in the shop and the table was always full. The tailors generally slept in the house too, and every room was filled with beds. There were only three bedrooms in the crowded house, so the attic was used as an additional sleeping quarter.

There was no electricity or running water in the home, although there was natural gas for cooking and lighting lamps. Oil and wood were available for burning too. But water had to be purchased and retrieved from the city spigot, and then carried home with two pails hung over a stick and poured into a large bucket for storage. Weekly bathing took place in a communal bathhouse, and a brick outhouse had to be used, which could get mighty cold during the winter.

Jacob felt that it was important for his sons to learn a trade. He assured them if they learned tailoring he could promise them two things: they would never be rich, and they would never be poor. Little did Michael and Sol know at the time that the tailoring skills they acquired would help them survive the war, as it gave them a valuable skill they were able to exchange for special treatment and essential provisions both inside and outside the concentration camps.

The tailor shop also provided occasions for the brothers to have contact with the non-Jewish population of Krosno that they might not otherwise have had. Research on helping behavior during the Holocaust has found that Christian Poles with prior relationships with Jews were more likely than those without such relationships to lend assistance.[9] Taduesz and Maria Duchowski, who later helped Sol pass as a Catholic, were customers of the Berger tailor shop who had had pleasant interactions with the family before the war.

Knowledge of non-Jewish culture, including language and religion, was also crucial to Jewish survival, particularly outside of the camps, in order to maintain a credible façade as a non-Jew. In prewar Poland more than half the Jewish children attended special Jewish schools that inhibited mastery of the Polish language. As boys, however, Michael and Sol attended public school in mixed classes and played with Catholic children. While the Berger family was by no means assimilated, the brothers acquired social skills that enabled them to interact effectively with non-Jews.

This is not to say that the brothers' relationship with the dominant Catholic population was always harmonious. Michael said that he had many Jewish as well as non-Jewish friends, but "our friendship with non-Jewish children was somewhat strained, alternating between being friendly and hostile." Fights during recess and after school were common, but the boys on both sides still played with each other every day.

Both Michael and Sol, like their father, were shorter than average, but they were tough.[10] Sol described himself as faring better than Michael in fights, while Michael recalled that he was often left alone because he was well liked. Sol seemed to hold more resentment about his childhood and recounted times when they rode their bicycles in the countryside and Polish kids would throw rocks at them while yelling "smell the Jews."

Both brothers expressed considerable acrimony toward the Polish teachers they had in school. Classes were held Monday through Saturday, and while the Jewish students were excused from attending classes on the Sabbath, some of the teachers intentionally chose Saturdays to teach new subjects in order to disadvantage the Jewish students. Upon returning to school on Monday, they would find themselves behind the other students and unable to complete homework that had been assigned in their absence.

Nonetheless, the two brothers were adept at picking up languages, a skill that was perhaps enhanced by the training in Hebrew they received through several years of Hebrew school, which prepared them for their bar mitzvahs when they were 13 years old. German was taught in school too, and through their interactions with Polish-Ukrainians, they picked up a dialect that was similar to Russian. These language skills would later come in handy during the war.

In prewar Poland, Jews who observed religious rules that dictated special rituals and dress often looked and behaved in ways that made them appear different from non-Jews. Orthodox Jewish men, for example, often grew long beards and sideburns that curled down to their shoulders, and they wore black hats and long black or gray caftans. During the war, these characteristics limited their ability to pass as Catholic Poles.

This observation should not be misconstrued as suggesting that Jews with strong religious commitments did not survive. Indeed, for many Jews such commitments were crucial in helping them endure their suffering. However, Michael's and Sol's religious views can be described as agnostic, although the Berger family did keep an Orthodox home and the boys retained a healthy respect for Jewish traditions. Michael said that "I never identified with the Orthodox view of Judaism, and on a daily basis, prayer and ritual meant very little to me." Similarly, Sol attended Hebrew school for two years past his bar mitzvah, "but later I just strayed." As boys their parents expected them to follow the Jewish tradition of keeping their heads covered, but they often removed their caps when outside of the home. With the exception of circumcision, there was nothing about their physical appearance or demeanor that would have prevented them from passing as Poles. For Sol, however, it was especially significant that he later learned about Catholicism while being locked in a jail cell with a Roman Catholic priest for several months during the early war years (for black market activities). This knowledge proved most valuable while trying to pass as a Catholic.

Although Jews were a minority that was discriminated against, Michael and Sol enjoyed all the normal activities of youth: playing soccer, ice skating, cross-country skiing, and swimming in the Wisłok River that flowed through the town. They also enjoyed summer vacations with their mother (their father was always working), and summer camp in the nearby mountains.

During their youth both brothers participated in Zionist youth groups, Michael in the left-wing Hashomer Hatzair and Sol in the right-wing Betar. Joshua was a member of a different left-wing Zionist group called Poale Zion; and Moses was a member of Agudat Israel, a Hasidic religious group that opposed the establishment of a Jewish state before the return of the Messiah. Although the parents were apolitical, the family dinner table was often the occasion for lively political debates. Sol thinks that he always won the debates, but admits that his brothers referred to him as a fascist, like the Italian dictator Benito Mussolini.

At that time Sol was more interested in Zionism than Judaism and even received paramilitary training from Betar with the intention of going to Palestine to fight for an independent Jewish state against the British, who controlled the area.[11] This ambition never materialized, but the training he received helped prepare him for his later wartime experience with the Polish partisans. As for Michael, he recalled how proud he was of the paramilitary training he received from a Polish Army officer in school, and how much he enjoyed the occasional sharpshooting with live ammunition. He also recalled marching with a pre-World War I vintage rifle, which was nearly as long as his body, in a military-style parade on Polish Independence Day.

Formal schooling in Poland ended with the seventh grade. Sol in particular wanted to go to high school, but slots were restricted for Jewish students. He applied for admission but was not accepted. Instead he enrolled in a private trade school with the intention of becoming a bookkeeper, but he couldn't find a job. When he was 16 years old, Sol also spent a year in Kraków.

He got a tailoring job to try to make ends meet, but was sometimes hungry. His mother sent him letters begging him to come back home. "It's time to come home. You have made your point," she wrote.

Life in Krosno went on without incident until September 1, 1939, when Germany invaded Poland. Things would never be the same.

The Berger family prior to Michael's birth (1921). Above (left to right): Bertha, Rosa, Sol. Below (left to right): Moses, Joshua, Jacob, Rose.

The extended Berger family (early 1930s), with Sol (above center) and Michael (below right).

The Berger brothers (left to right): Michael, Sol, Joshua, Moses.

Children, Save Yourselves!

The Berger tailor shop (late 1930s), with Michael (bottom, second to left) and Sol (back left).

Michael (late 1930s).   *Sol (late 1930s).*

2

The Invasion

At about 5:00 A.M. on September 1, 1939, the Berger family was awakened by heavy explosions as the German Air Force bombed the Polish airfield located on the outskirts of Krosno. The Polish planes were destroyed before they had a chance to leave the ground. Hours later the Polish radio announced that German troops manning motorized tanks had crossed the Polish border and were advancing toward Krosno.

The Polish Army that had been deployed to the western front was no match for the German Army and began retreating. Prior to the invasion, Joshua, who had completed a term of duty in the military in the latter part of 1938, had already been re-called to active duty. Now all young men of military age were ordered to follow the army to the east.

Michael and Sol, along with a group of their friends, packed a few clothes and started a long march on foot into eastern Poland. They walked for several days covering more than 200 kilometers, occasionally dodging machine-gun fire from low-flying German planes by jumping into ditches along the side of the road as bullets flew all around them.

A few days into their journey, traveling off the main highway, they saw German tanks in the area of Poland that is now Ukraine. They met up with some Polish soldiers who were roaming the countryside without leadership. The war had been lost and there was no longer a reason for the young men to continue further. They entered a small farm, where they bought some food and spent the night sleeping in the barn.

The following morning Michael and Sol's group started their walk back home. There were thousands of people going in all directions. Everybody wanted to be reunited with their families. The Ukrainians felt liberated by the Germans, who granted them police powers, and they were committing atrocities against Poles, especially Jews. In light of this situation, the Berger brothers and their friends decided it would be safer to act as if they were non-Jewish Poles. Several times they were stopped by German soldiers. They didn't know what to expect from the Germans, but they had heard that the Germans were harassing Jews and even killing them right on the spot.

Very few Poles spoke German, but since Sol spoke a little, they chose him as their spokesman. The Germans questioned them about who they were and where they were going. Speaking in broken German, Sol explained that they had been separated from their families and were returning home. He told them that they were German nationals who had been living in Poland for generations and had escaped from the Polish authorities when they wanted to draft them into the Polish Army to fight Germany. Fortunately, the Germans believed the story and let them go.

One time they were stopped and searched by German soldiers. Michael had a metal cigarette case in the inside pocket of his coat, and the soldier who searched him thought he was armed. The soldier pulled out his gun, pointed it at Michael's head, and told him to take it out. Fearing for his life, Michael pulled out the cigarette case and handed it to the soldier. The soldier kept it and sent them on their way.

The young men reached the town of Sanok, about 35 kilometers east of Krosno, where they entered a school building to spend the night. The Germans had issued a curfew order and informed the people that civilians seen out after dark would be shot. In the late evening they were visited by a German officer who questioned them. Sol appeared to convince him of their story; the officer was friendly and promised to return in the morning at 7:00 A.M. to provide them with transportation back home. Wisely they didn't trust the German and left by 6:00 A.M.

When they arrived in Krosno, Michael and Sol were excited to be reunited with their family. They hadn't slept in a bed for about two weeks, and it felt great to be home! But Joshua hadn't returned, and they were worried about him. The Geheime Staatspolizei, or Gestapo, the Nazi secret police in charge of political offenses, including Jewish matters, had arrived on the heels of the German Army and established a command office less than a block from their home. The family had heard of the Gestapo's reputation for terrorizing the population, and they expected them to be especially hard on Jews.

When Germany invaded Poland, it was impossible for anyone to know exactly what the Nazis had in store for the Jews. Jews had been subject to discrimination for centuries, and many viewed their experience during the early war years as a modern version of older persecutions. No one could have imagined that they intended to exterminate an entire group of people!

Prior to the invasion, Adolf Hitler had signed a pact with

Children, Save Yourselves!

Joseph Stalin, the leader of the Soviet Union, to partition Poland into a German side and a Soviet side. A border was established on the San River about 40 kilometers east of Krosno, and by the end of the month the Gestapo began encouraging Jews to move to the Soviet side. But transportation was not provided and means of survival were unsure.

All signs indicated that it would be better to live under the Russians than the Germans. The Berger family decided that it would be too difficult for all of them, especially Jacob and Rosa, to leave. Moses did not want to go, and Bertha and her husband, Rafael Jakubowicz, had two young daughters, Sonia (age 11) and Mania (age 7), to look after. The family still hadn't learned what happened to Joshua—whether he was alive, a war prisoner, or killed on the front—and wanted to wait for his return. Nonetheless, Jacob and Rosa encouraged Michael and Sol to depart. Jacob told his sons, "Don't worry about your mother and me. Just take care of yourself. I wish nothing more but for *you* to get through this."

After a tearful parting, Michael and Sol joined up with a few of their friends and started their way on foot to Soviet-occupied Poland. They crossed the San River and spent a few days in a small border village. From there they took a train further east to Sambor, a medium-sized city in eastern Poland about 140 kilometers from Krosno. The brothers' first impression of the Soviet occupation was fairly favorable. They didn't detect any anti-Semitism among the soldiers, and they thought that if they were going to be occupied by a foreign army, they much preferred the Russians to the Germans. Still, they felt like orphans and missed their family very much.

Michael and Sol slept in a vacated schoolhouse for a few nights and in a community building for refugees. As they were running low on food and money, they began looking around for ways to make money. They knew how to speak a little Ukrainian and were able to communicate reasonably well with the Russian soldiers. There was a shortage of goods in the stores, and a black market was flourishing. Everyone was buying and selling to the troops, who were sending everything they could—from dry goods to jewelry—back to their homes. Michael and Sol soon realized that the Russian standard of living even lagged behind prewar Poland's. Although the soldiers seemed to have plenty of money and were eager to spend it, there were few commodities available in the Soviet Union to buy.

The brothers were amused by the wives of the Soviet officers, who had never seen a nightgown before. They wore these nightgowns in public, thinking they were fancy evening dresses. The Russians were especially desirous of watches, sometimes even if they did not work (thinking they could get them repaired). Michael recalled a time when an officer approached him and asked how much he wanted for a watch. Michael quoted him a price, but the officer wanted to confirm that it worked. Michael shook the watch, got it to run, and put it to the Russian's ear. The officer gave him the money and hurried off thinking he had gotten a bargain.

About a month after arriving in Sambor, Michael met a young Jewish woman about his age who took the brothers home to meet her parents. The parents owned a grocery store and had no problem supplying themselves with food; there was very little meat, but plenty of bread and potatoes. They invited Michael and Sol to stay with them for a while.

The brothers began looking around for other ways to make money. Sol got a job as a tailor to supplement their income. They also learned about goods that could be bought in Lwów, a larger city about 75 kilometers away, and they began making trips there by train. Michael recalled watching for lines of people, and wherever there was a line, he would get in it, not even knowing what they were selling. One time he stood in line all night, and when they opened the store in the morning, he discovered they were selling material for suits and other clothing. He bought three and one-half yards of nice wool cloth, enough to make a man's suit. It cost him about 70 złotys, and he sold it back in Sambor for 190.

One day as Michael and Sol were boarding the train to Lwów, they heard their names called out. They turned around and saw their missing brother Joshua still in his Polish uniform! He had been taken prisoner by the Soviet Army and was being marched east toward Soviet Russia when he managed to escape and get on a train headed west. They were overwhelmed with happiness and wished they could let their parents know that Joshua was alive and well. But there was no way to communicate with them because there was no mail delivery between the Soviet and German sides of the divide.

On another day, Michael and a couple of his friends heard that the Soviet authorities were registering Poles in Lwów for work in the coal mines in eastern Russia. They stood outside all night in the freezing cold to wait for the registration office to open. In the morning a Soviet officer who was Jewish spoke to them in Yiddish.[1] He accepted Michael's friends, who were 6 feet tall, but wouldn't take Michael because he was too short. The officer told him that he wasn't strong enough and "wouldn't last a week."

Upon returning to Sambor, Michael developed a bad cold, flu, and heavy cough—it was probably pneumonia. Sol and Joshua decided that he needed the care of their mother and the comforts of home, and they didn't want the responsibility of looking after a sick sibling. But it had become more difficult to cross the border back into the German side of Poland, because the tensions between Germany and the Soviet Union were mounting. The brothers had learned that there were Poles (mostly farmers) who would smuggle Jews across the San River for a fee. They hired a Pole to take Michael and another Krosno youth they had met across. Three to four weeks later, Sol and Joshua hired a smuggler to take them across too. They crossed the river on New Year's Eve, when they assumed that the soldiers on both sides of the border would be partying. They planned to persuade the entire family that it was time for all of them to move to the Soviet side.

In retrospect, Michael and Sol think it was a mistake to have returned home. Their parents were elated to see them and to learn that Joshua was alive, but the atmosphere in Krosno was much more repressive than when they had left.[2] The Gestapo was on every corner, and Jews had been ordered to wear armbands marked with the Star of David to prevent them from mingling with or hiding among the non-Jewish population. The family was now prepared to abandon everything—their home and personnel possessions—to flee. But they wanted to wait for the weather to get warmer to make traveling easier. This was not to be. The borders were being guarded more closely, and it became impossible to cross over to the Soviet side.

Children, Save Yourselves!

3

The Occupation

By the end of October 1939, the Nazis established the General Government throughout Poland. The General Government was the administrative unit that placed all of Poland that had not been formally incorporated into Germany or that was not part of Soviet territory under direct German rule. In Krosno, as in other communities, the Gestapo exercised primary control, although non-Gestapo police and military personnel were present as well.

Gustav Schmatzler, the chief Gestapo officer in Krosno, ruled with vicious and arbitrary authority. At times everything could seem to be going smoothly, without incident. Jews would be allowed to go about their daily business, attend synagogue, and hold prayer meetings. The next minute there would be a raid, and people would be rounded up and disappear, never to be seen again. This inconsistency confused the Jews, deterring them from trying to hide or escape, and giving them false hope that their plight might only be temporary.

A key element of German rule over the Jews throughout Europe was the Judenräte, or Jewish Councils. The Councils were set up by the Nazis to administer their edicts and manage the Jewish population for them. They coordinated the provision of social services (including food, housing, and medical needs) as if they were city governments, but at the Nazis' behest, they also arranged for the confiscation of Jewish valuables and selected Jews for forced labor and even transport to concentration camps.

In Krosno, a Jewish Council was established in early 1940 under the leadership of Judah Engel, a Krosno native who had lived for many years in Germany before being deported back to Poland. The Council created a Jewish police force and several departments to cope with growing problems, such as arrival of about 500 indigent Jews whom the Nazis had relocated from Łódź.

Michael recalled several occasions in which he socialized with Łódź Jews in the company of a German police officer. Most of the Łódź Jews lived in the synagogue, but some managed to get rooms with local families. There was one family—a father, mother, and two attractive daughters—that was protected by this officer because he liked the girls. Michael and his friends would visit their home and enjoy singing, storytelling, and reading books together—all in the company of this officer. He recalled one young woman from Łódź who had a number of German admirers. She spent many nights in the homes of the Germans, who lavished her with gifts, even though it was a capital offense for Jews and Germans to have sexual relations with each other. It always amazed Michael how the Germans could be fond of some of the Jewish women at the same time that they were willing to abuse or kill the rest of them. This paradox was part of this inconsistent treatment that kept Jews off guard, and

Michael thought the Germans did this purposely to confuse and delude them.

Sol also described an incident when his brothers and he were working at the airfield under the supervision of a German Air Force sergeant that had an outcome one wouldn't have expected. The Jews were carrying heavy boards—two men on each end of the board and one in the center. His brother Moses, whom Sol described as lazy, was in the center not doing his part, slumping down below the board so it didn't rest on his shoulder. The sergeant, who was a large man, saw this, pulled Moses aside, and started berating and beating him. Sol reacted without thinking. "Leave him alone," he told the sergeant. "Why is it any of your business?" the sergeant replied. "You're hitting my brother," Sol said. Then, when the sergeant gave Sol a push, Sol punched him hard in the face, stretching him out on the ground. The sergeant was of course startled that a Jew would do such a thing. He got up and pulled out his gun as if to shoot Sol. But for some reason he changed his mind and just said, "Go back to work!" Looking back, Sol does not understand why the sergeant didn't shoot him on the spot. "I was a tough young man," Sol said. "But it was a stupid thing to do."

Nevertheless, with each new day the iron hand of the Gestapo tightened over the Jewish community. Daily the Nazis instructed the Jewish Council to deliver a certain number of Jews for forced labor. They worked at the airfield, shoveled snow from the highways, cleaned the city streets, and loaded and unloaded coal at the train depot. They worked 10 to 12 grueling hours a day. Some Jews who possessed special skills—like electricians, automotive repairmen, carpenters, shoemakers, and tailors—were treated a little better because the Germans required their services. Since the Bergers owned their own tailor shop and many Germans, including Gestapo officials, enjoyed their free services, for a while they did not suffer as much as other Jewish families.

One day Sol told the family that he was thinking of joining the Jewish police force. "It'll help the family," he explained. But the rest of the family opposed this. Jacob put his foot down: "No one in this family is going to collaborate with the Nazis!" he exclaimed. "I don't care what privileges you think you'll get." Michael recalled being resentful of the Jews who did such things: "I suppose you can't blame them for wanting to minimize the hardship for themselves and their families. But this type of cooperation went against my grain. You never knew what kind of dirty work you'd have to do. There was one boy, the son of a Jewish baker, who became a policeman. He was forced to put his own father on a truck for deportation! I would never have joined them."

Although no one in the Berger family attempted to flee or go into hiding, they did resist Nazi edicts whenever they could. When the Gestapo ordered the Jews to turn over all pieces of jewelry, gold, and silver, Rosa objected, in spite of the fact that anyone found disobeying such orders could be immediately shot.

Rosa owned a large silver candelabra, which had taken her many years of saving to buy. It had been every Jewish woman's ambition to own such a candelabra for the lighting of candles on the Sabbath. Rosa couldn't bring herself to turn it over to the Germans, so she gave it to a Catholic friend, Maria Duchowski, assuming Maria would eventually return it.

A week later the Gestapo demanded that the Jews hand over all articles made of copper, which the Germans recycled and used for war materials. The only item the Bergers owned was a bean grinder they used to make coffee; they delivered this to the Gestapo. Next the Gestapo demanded all furs, including fur collars that had to be torn off from their coats; these items were sent to Germany to be used for German military personnel and civilians. The following day, Jews could be seen wearing their coats without collars. As she had done with her candelabra, Rosa gave her coat to a girlfriend.

After the deadline for delivering fur materials had passed, the Bergers realized they hadn't turned over a fur vest they owned. So they decided to burn it in their old wood-burning oven. It was a winter night and the stench of the burning vest was noticeable outside. The Gestapo headquarters was just down the street, and the family was very anxious about being discovered, fearing that this little act of defiance could cost them their lives.

Perhaps inspired by their parents' fortitude, but going against their wishes, Michael and Sol often disregarded the armband order. Although noncompliance was punishable by death, they would remove their armbands and ride their bicycles or take a train to nearby towns to visit relatives or make transactions on the black market. In spite of their defiant attitude, however, they always feared being recognized by Poles, many of whom reported Jews to the Gestapo. This they did for reward money or plain anti-Semitism. As Michael recalled, "The Germans in their cunning way were successful at dividing the population. The propaganda newspapers had convinced many of the Poles that the Jews were the cause of the war and that they had lost their country because of an international Jewish conspiracy."[1]

One time Michael and a friend rode their bicycles to the nearby town of Rymanów, about 16 kilometers away, to buy pepper on the black market. They arranged a purchase of two 25 kilogram sacks (about 55 pounds each) at a tavern owned by Rosa's uncle. As they were getting ready to leave the next day, a Polish-Ukrainian police officer appeared. Someone had apparently reported them to the officer, because when he started questioning them, it was obvious that he knew what Michael and his friend were doing. This officer, however, had a reputation for taking bribes. He threatened to arrest them, but when the uncle offered him a beer and then some money, he left them alone. Michael and his friend loaded the sacks of pepper onto their bikes and rode back to Krosno. When they returned, they sold the pepper to another black marketeer for a profit.

Sol, too, had dealings in the black market. One incident in November 1940, though dangerous, initiated a series of events that exposed him to valuable cultural knowledge that later helped him survive. Sol took a train to the city of Tarnów, about 80 kilometers away, to buy U.S. dollars with Polish złotys from a dollar dealer. Sol's intention was to acquire enough U.S. currency to pay for boat tickets for about a dozen young Zionists who intended to escape Poland to Romania, where they planned to book passage to sail on the Black Sea toward Palestine.

When Sol arrived in Tarnów, he ran into a Jewish friend whom he had known from a Betar training camp. The friend asked Sol what he was doing in Tarnów, and Sol told him he was there to buy dollars. The friend asked Sol when he would be leaving to go home, and Sol told him he was going back on the afternoon train. The friend said he would return to see him off.

Later, when Sol arrived at the station, his friend was there to greet him. But after they said their goodbyes and parted ways, a plainclothes Gestapo officer walked over to Sol and arrested him. Sol suspected that his so-called friend was an informer and that he had pointed him out to the Gestapo, because there was no other reason for the officer to stop him.

The officer searched Sol for the dollars, but Sol had been careful not to carry them on his person. The dollar dealer had sent his 12-year-old daughter along, and she was carrying the money. The girl was supposed to hand the money to Sol just before he boarded the train, but when the Gestapo arrested Sol, he arrested her too. Later Sol learned that the officer had confiscated the money and released the girl so there would be no record of her arrest.

At the jailhouse Sol was interrogated by two Gestapo officers who beat him mercilessly for more than two hours. Sol was defiant and would not admit that he had purchased any U.S. money or that he knew anyone involved in anti-German activity. Finally the officers said, "That's enough for today. We'll start again tomorrow." They left Sol on the floor, black and blue all over and temporarily deaf from the blows he had received to the sides of his head.

Sol was locked in a second-story room with an iron-barred window that had a circle in the middle that faced the street. He was very thin at the time and was able to put his head through the center and squeeze his body through the hole. Without a coat—it was winter and very cold—he slid down the gutter to the street and ran, not knowing where to go. He spotted a young woman on the street wearing a Jewish armband and approached her, asking if she would take him to her home. She agreed to help him, and the family was kind enough to let him hide out in their house for a couple of weeks. He wore women's clothes and even a wig—it was common for women to wear wigs back then—just in case. He also sent word to his parents to let them know where he was.

Eventually, Rosa let Sol know that she had passed a bribe through a cousin, Felix Gebel, who had connections with the Gestapo, and that it was safe to come home. But unbeknownst to them, Gebel never passed on the money, and when Sol arrived home, a Gestapo official named Oscar Becker was waiting to arrest him.

Becker was a notorious figure, nicknamed the "Terrible Phantom" because he would appear unannounced and kill Jews for no apparent reason. He did know the Berger family, because they had made clothes for him, so perhaps he took kindly to them and decided not to kill anyone that day.

But Becker did take Sol back to Gestapo headquarters and brought him before chief officer Schmatzler. Schmatzler looked at Sol and asked Becker, rhetorically, "That's him?" He then asked Sol, "What did you do that they arrested you and you escaped?" Sol replied, "I don't know. I was just stopped without any reason. I was beaten up and just couldn't take it. When I got a chance, I escaped." Matter-of-factly, Schmatzler told Sol, "Well, you won't do it again."

Sol was not sure whether Schmatzler actually knew why he'd been arrested in Tarnów, but he did have an order to rearrest Sol. Schmatzler was very polite, but put Sol in handcuffs, escorted him to a car, and drove him to the nearby town of Jasło, where he was jailed without a hearing.

When Sol first arrived at the prison, German guards ordered him to take off his clothes. They sprayed him with disinfectant for lice, made him take a cold shower, and gave him thin prison clothes to wear.

He was placed in a large cell with 11 other Polish prisoners, including a Roman Catholic priest who had resisted the German occupation. Sol was the only Jew among them. The cell had straw sacks to sleep on and a tiny barred window that was too high to see outside. There was no running water or toilet—just one bucket for drinking water and one for toileting. The prisoners were allowed out of their cells just one day per week, when the guards ushered them into the prison courtyard and let them walk silently for 15 minutes.

During the day, Sol did squats and sit-ups to keep in shape, but the food rations were sparse and he began to lose weight. Occasionally the prisoners received small packages from home; Rosa sent Sol pieces of bread and fruit. But most of what was sent was stolen by the prison trustees. Once a month they were taken to cold communal showers that did not always have soap.

As it turned out, however, Sol's arrest was a fortuitous event, because he learned about religious rituals that would later help him pass as a Catholic. Sol paid close attention as the priest conducted rituals three times a day. He memorized the

Lord's Prayer and the Hail Mary prayer. He learned how to properly make the sign of the cross and take Communion, which the priest conducted with bread rather than wafers and water rather than wine.

After being incarcerated for six months, Sol was called into the prison office where he was met by a German officer, not a Gestapo official, who said he was in charge of foreign currencies. He read Sol a document that said he'd been dealing in dollars, that he had been arrested by the Gestapo in Tarnów, and that he had escaped and been rearrested. The officer wanted Sol to sign a confession.

Sol was worried about what would happen to him if he admitted guilt. So he told the officer that the charges were false. The officer replied that for every lie Sol told, he would receive 25 blows to his back with a rubber club. Sol continued to refuse, and the officer ordered him to lie down. The officer then struck Sol 25 times as he counted each blow out loud. Following the beating, Sol relented and admitted he'd been arrested and escaped. But he insisted that he hadn't been dealing in dollars, upon which the officer struck him another 25 times.

All told, the officer counted to 25 four times, after which he said that if Sol wouldn't sign the confession, he would send him back to his cell indefinitely. Sol asked him what would happen if he signed. The officer said he would be released to his mother who was waiting outside. Finally, Sol gave in and signed the confession. He was returned to his cell and immediately passed out. The next day he was released. When he got home, he learned that Rosa had arranged to pay off the Gestapo in exchange for his release if he signed a confession.

Thus far in their ordeal, the Berger family had managed to stay together and avoid the most severe consequences of the Nazi occupation. But more difficult and traumatic times were soon to come.

4

Children, Save Yourselves!

O n June 22, 1941, Germany launched Operation Barbarossa, breaking its nonaggression pact with the Soviet Union and pushing the Soviet Army beyond Polish territory into Soviet Russia.[1] It also was at this time that the Nazis escalated their murderous campaign against the Jews and moved toward implementing the Final Solution, their systematic program of extermination.[2] The Einsatsgruppen, the mobile military units of the Schutzstafel, better known as the SS, were tasked with killing civilians. The Einsatsgruppen followed the German Army into Soviet-controlled territory. After the army secured the area, the Einsatsgruppen murdered thousands of civilian Jews and Gentiles.[3]

In Krosno, random raids and deportations became more common. People were executed in open daylight on city streets.

No German official needed any justification for killing Polish civilians, especially Jews. Each dispensed justice according to his own mood or whim.

In May 1942, as the Final Solution was fully underway, the Gestapo ordered the creation of the Krosno ghetto in a one block area on Franciszkanska Street that had been used as an egg and poultry market known as the "egg place." Alex White, a survivor from Krosno, estimates that about 4,000 Jews, whose ranks had been swelled by refugees from other villages and towns, were ordered into the ghetto.[4] A gate patrolled by armed guards regulated movement in and out of the area, and Jews needed a special permit or work order to leave.

The Berger family received a temporary reprieve from the ghetto relocation order because the Nazis still valued their tailoring services and allowed them to remain in their home. Organisation Todt, a German agency in charge of military supplies, enlisted the Bergers to make uniforms for German troops.[5] They didn't pay them with money, but they did give them food—mostly cereals and bread, and occasionally meat.

On August 9, 1942, the Nazis issued an order for all the Krosno Jews, regardless of age, gender, or health, to report the following morning at the Targowica, a large plaza near the railway station that was used as a cattle marketplace, for "registration." Each Jew was allowed to bring up to 10 kilograms (about 22 pounds) of personal possessions. Homes and apartments were to remain unlocked and available for police inspection. Anyone found in their homes after 9:00 A.M. would be shot on sight. Panic erupted! Some people tried to escape, but most of them were caught and shot, mostly by Polish-Ukrainian troops known as Hiwis (Hilfswilligen or volunteers) who had been trained by the SS.

The next morning the Berger family gathered to walk to the marketplace. Among them were Jacob and Rosa; the brothers Michael, Sol, Joshua, and Moses; sister Bertha and her husband, Rafael, and their daughters, Sonia and Mania.

As the people assembled in the marketplace, trucks with SS, Gestapo, German police, and Hiwis arrived and encircled the area so that no one could escape. The Gestapo ordered the Jews to line up in rows of four, with men in one group and women and children in another group, to get ready for "registration."[6] The orders were translated into Polish through the Jewish Council.

Sol recalled a Gestapo officer with a baton who walked around the marketplace pointing to the older and disabled people, ordering them to step out of the line and stand to one side. Alex White recalled an SS officer with a whip who did the same. Once again, panic erupted, as the assembled wailed and wept! Local Catholic Poles gathered around to watch the spectacle.

Jacob realized what was happening and told his sons, "This is the end for me. Nobody comes back from these transports. But you must make me a promise! Survive any way you can. Don't be a hero. Just survive to tell the story about what happened."

Jacob was segregated with the other elderly who were escorted by Hiwis and police into the back of the trucks. Some of them were brutally beaten, and those unable to climb onto the trucks on their own were simply picked up and thrown on top of the others. One younger woman stepped out of line to plead with a Gestapo officer to release her elderly mother. He ordered the woman onto the truck with her mother. She continued to plead with him but to no avail.

As Jacob boarded the truck, he turned and shouted, "CHILDREN, SAVE YOURSELVES!" This was the last thing he said to his sons. In many ways, it was a poignant gift, for in *his* moment of death, Jacob helped his sons maintain *their* will to live. And it is perhaps for this reason that Michael and Sol, in spite of their profound grief over the loss of their parents, never felt the pangs of "survivor guilt." As Michael said, "It wouldn't do the dead any good, and it's not what my father would have wanted."

The trucks departed under heavily armed guard, with machine guns mounted on accompanying vehicles. Those remaining in the marketplace were forced to stand. Anyone who sat down was beaten or shot. A few hours later the trucks, now empty, returned to Krosno. All but the most naïve realized they had likely been machine-gunned to death.

There were still many people remaining in the marketplace, however. Representatives of various German military services arrived and selected a group of young people whom they needed for forced labor and skilled work, mostly in the airfield. An Organisation Todt official asked and received permission from the Gestapo to release the four Berger brothers, Rafael, and Sonia (who looked older than her age) to work under his supervision. The brothers pleaded with the Todt official to allow Rosa, Bertha, and their younger niece Mania to come with them, but he refused. They were left behind as the rest of the family was taken to work in a Todt supply warehouse.

That night the (temporarily) fortunate members of the Berger family were taken to the Franciszkanska Street ghetto, where they were required to register for a work permit. According to Michael's recollection, the ghetto consisted of four houses, two three-story apartments, and one single-story apartment crowded with about 15 to 20 people per room. People slept on the floor and three high on wooden bunk beds. Michael recalled that the conditions were "incredibly bad. Everything had been taken away from us. We were overwhelmed with grief! My heart ached! I could not sleep. All we had was a temporary reprieve for ourselves and the hope that we might survive."

The next morning the four Berger brothers, now separated from Rafael and Sonia, were led under armed guard to work in the family's tailor shop, which was now managed by a Pole, to make uniforms for Organisation Todt and civilian clothes for the personal use of the chief Todt official and his wife.

They also learned through the grapevine about what had happened to the Jews who had remained in the marketplace after they had left, including Rosa, Bertha, and Mania. The poor souls had been standing all day, dehydrated from the heat, with no water to drink, and many were severely beaten. At the end of the day they were led to the railway station and loaded into closed freight cars with about 60 people per car. Dr. Jakob Baumring, a prominent Jewish physician and a member of the Jewish Council, called out from the train, "You are barbarians!" The guards dragged him from the car and shot him right on the spot. The train left eastward the next morning for the concentration camp at Bełżec, about 190 kilometers away. When they arrived, they were immediately gassed.

◆ ◆ ◆

Historian Martin Gilbert estimates that about 79,200 Jews were deported to Bełżec in August 1942, 5,000 from the Krosno area alone.[7] Those who survived that month in Krosno were not an entirely random group. They were largely a cohort of younger people, who, like the Berger brothers, were deemed suitable for work. In the early part of September, however, the Gestapo ordered the Krosno Jewish Council to deliver all the remaining Jewish tailors for transport to an SS military camp at Moderówka, about 13 kilometers away, where they were expected to work making uniforms for Hiwi troops. At first the Berger brothers refused to comply and tried to convince the Council to allow them to remain in Krosno. In a heated exchange, with Sol taking the lead, they told the Council that they still had a lot of work to complete for various German officials. The Council, now headed by Moshe Kleiner, insisted that they were under orders to deliver 30 Jewish tailors. After calling Sol a "hund schwein" (dog hog), Kleiner shouted, "That's enough! Two of you can stay to finish the work and two of you will report for transport tomorrow morning!"

The brothers had a family meeting to decide who would go and who would stay. They realized that it made sense for Sol and Joshua to remain. They were the most skilled tailors, and Sol had a Jewish friend, Jan Nagel, who had ties to a Jewish printer who was now working for the Gestapo and had access to official seals. Apparently this printer had made himself an extra seal that he used to stamp forged documents, which he made available to Jews. The plan was for Michael and Moses to go to Moderówka, and for Sol and Joshua to try to get stamped false identity papers with Polish surnames and somehow smuggle them into the camp. Then they would all try to escape by any means they could. The next day, Michael and Moses were taken away, and it was at that point that Michael's and Sol's survival trajectories for the rest of the war took dramatically different turns.

◆ ◆ ◆

After Michael's and Moses's departure, Sol and Joshua continued their routine of working in the tailor shop, laboring six days a week from morning to night, returning to the ghetto to sleep. Most of the other Jews in the ghetto received only a small ration of black bread twice a day to eat, but Sol and Joshua were fortunate to receive extra food at the shop. Occasionally Maria Duchowski, Rosa's friend, also came to the tailor shop to bring them extra food. She gave them blankets and pillows for sleeping too.

In early December, Sol and Joshua noticed additional Gestapo and SS personnel arriving in town. They suspected that something ominous was about to happen. Jan Nagel told them he had learned about plans to liquidate the ghetto.

Sol and Joshua had heard about anti-Nazi Polish partisans who were hiding out in the nearby forests. They did not know their exact location, but with the false identity papers they had acquired from Jan—they had been unable to get them for Michael and Moses—they planned to escape and join them.

While Sol waited at the tailor shop, Joshua went back to the ghetto to retrieve some warmer clothing—it was freezing cold outside—and some extra food. Sol waited until just before nightfall, but Joshua did not return. He knew he had to act quickly before he was expected back at the ghetto. Cautiously he walked to the home of the Duchowskis, about five minutes away. He knocked on the door and asked if he could stay overnight. Maria's husband, Taduesz, was not there; he was working as a supervisor with a Polish construction crew rebuilding bridges for the Germans in Niźniów and Czortków, two towns located about 350 to 400 kilometers, respectively, to the east. Maria agreed to let Sol stay.[8]

The following morning of December 4, 1942, Maria went out to see what was happening. The final liquidation of the Krosno Jews was underway. People were being beaten and shot dead in the streets! For the last time in Krosno, panic erupted as the ghetto was cleared and everyone who was not killed was loaded onto trucks and driven to a larger ghetto in Rzeszów, about 60 kilometers away. Most of them eventually perished. Although we do not know for sure, Joshua was likely among them.

Sol told Maria of his plan to escape into the forest and join up with the partisans, and that he had acquired a false identity card that identified him as Jan Jerzowski to help him get by. He also had a false Organisation Todt work order indicating he was expected to report to work near the city of Kiev about 740 kilometers to the east in the Ukraine.

Children, Save Yourselves!

But Maria said she had a better idea. She told him to go to see her husband in Czortków and ask him for help. She wrote the address where Taduesz was staying on a piece of paper and told Sol to memorize it and destroy the paper.

Over the next couple of days, while Sol hid in Maria's attic, the Gestapo and SS searched the community for hiding Jews. Fortunately for Sol, for the most part they did not search the homes of Catholic Poles. On the third day, Maria told Sol it was safe to leave and that she would accompany him to the train station at the neighboring town of Iwonicz, about 11 kilometers away.

In the evening they walked for two hours through snow-covered fields, as Sol's boots and socks became soaked from the snow. At the dimly lit and unguarded Iwonicz train station, Maria purchased a train ticket for Sol, wished him good luck, and said goodbye. Sol waited behind a building for an hour until the train arrived. In his pocket he carried several tablets of arsenic, which he intended to swallow if captured. Sol said that he preferred to take his own life than give "the Germans the satisfaction of killing me." When the train arrived, Sol boarded and headed east.

5

Passing

The train on which Sol was traveling during his escape from Krosno made its first stop at the town of Drohobycz, about 160 kilometers to the east. The passengers were told to deboard and wait six or seven hours before boarding another train to continue their journey.

It was very cold, with lots of snow on the ground, and Sol's boots and socks were still a bit wet. He decided to look for a place inside where he could wait. He began walking and came upon a young man about his age who was wearing an armband with the Star of David. Sol asked if there was a Jewish ghetto and if it was possible to get in and out. The man told Sol to follow him.

They arrived at a ghetto, which was fenced but still easy to get through. Poles were coming and going—conducting business, bringing in food, and buying goods from the Jews. Sol and the young man went inside an apartment full of bunk beds. Sol took his shoes and socks off to dry and the occupants gave him some food.

After about four hours, Sol walked back to the train station, accompanied by the young man. Sol thanked him and said goodbye, and the man give him some parting words of encouragement: "I want to tell you that you are going to survive the war. If I didn't recognize you as a Jew, nobody else will either."

Once the train departed, a Ukrainian police officer began walking down the aisle asking the passengers for identification. Sol handed him his Jan Jerzowski card. The officer looked at it and asked Sol to recite the Lord's Prayer. Sol had memorized the prayer while imprisoned in Jasło and was able to recite it without hesitation. The officer was satisfied, returned the card, and continued down the aisle

The train stopped in the city of Stanisławów, about 260 kilometers from Krosno, where the passengers had to deboard because the main bridges were out. They were transported by horse and buggy across a temporary bridge and boarded another train to Czortków, where Taduesz Duchowski was living. Sol located his residence, a small house, but Taduesz was not home. Sol waited for him to return.

Research indicates that in most cases, Christian aid to Jews during the war had an unplanned beginning, and this was certainly true of Taduesz.[1] It was not something he had previously thought of or anticipated doing, but he responded to a situational demand from a person who was in peril of being killed.

When Taduesz arrived, Sol asked, "Excuse me, sir. Do you recognize me?" At first Taduesz did not; he had patronized the Berger tailor shop and knew Jacob better than his sons. Taduesz said, "No, I'm sorry, I don't know you. But you do look familiar." Then Sol said, "You might not remember *me*, but you do remember my *father*," and he proceeded to explain why he had come to see him and how Maria had said Taduesz might help.

Taduesz took Sol to a local restaurant and tried to figure out what he could do. He knew it would be dangerous to help Sol, but he agreed to do what he could. Taduesz was a supervisor in his construction company's office and offered to give Sol cover as a worker, as long as Sol understood that he couldn't be put on the payroll. Sol told him he had money saved from his black market activities—about 50 $1 bills—and would be most grateful for anything he could do.

Taduesz told Sol there were a lot of Ukrainian police in Czortków and that the Gestapo had a training school for Poles of German descent. He explained that nearby Niźniów, which was a smaller town, would be safer. There were a number of Ukrainian police there too, but the chances of running into someone who would recognize Sol would be less.

Taduesz took Sol to the Niźniów police station and helped him register as a company worker and get a food ration card. Taduesz introduced Sol to the attending officer, handed him Sol's fake identification card, and said, "This is Jan Jerzowski. He was sent from western Poland to work on the bridge. He needs to be registered." The officer asked Sol where he was living, and Sol said he was currently looking for a place. The officer recorded his name in a ledger and said to come back when he had secured a residence.

Taduesz then took Sol to the construction office and introduced him to the staff. One person told Sol of a place where he could rent an inexpensive room from another worker. He walked Sol over to the house and introduced him to the owner, who lived alone and was glad to have the company. After settling in, Sol returned to the police station to register his address.

Sol's subsequent experiences in Niźniów involved working in the company office and going out on location to the bridge every day—looking busy, making notes and charts, and trying to appear important. In addition to trading his dollars for local currency, he also did some tailoring for office employees to make extra money.

Sol learned that the man in charge of the office was the son of a judge who was a Jew who had converted to Catholicism. The son was likely raised as a Christian, but by German criteria he was still Jewish. The people in the office knew who he was, but no one said anything. One day this man said to Sol, "Let's go for a walk." He looked at Sol suspiciously and said, "Tell me, are you ... ?" He didn't even finish his sentence. Sol said, "Am I what?" The man was evasive and Sol said, "Are you?" They were both uncomfortable, and neither of them admitted what they suspected of each other—that they were both Jewish or of Jewish descent.

Sol felt that he knew more about this man than he knew about Sol, but eventually the man told him, "Let me give you some advice." He said that Sol should be careful about his pronunciation of certain Polish words, because he wasn't articulating them properly, and that he shouldn't put a sugar cube in his mouth when he drank tea or coffee, or eat sunflower seeds, because these were Jewish customs. Later Taduesz told this man to leave Sol alone or his own life would be in danger.

Meanwhile, Sol lived as a Catholic and concealed his identity to everyone but Taduesz. He attended Mass every day, as did the other practicing Catholics, and applied what he had learned about Catholicism. He never dared go to Confession, however, because he had never observed the sacrament and didn't know what to do. On several occasions the priest asked Sol about coming to Confession. Sol put him off by saying he had confessed in a neighboring town and that he would confess again soon.

During this time Sol befriended a Polish woman named Kristina whom he met at church. Kristina had been a schoolteacher, but the Nazis had closed the school. She and Sol came to an understanding that they were both Polish patriots and anti-Nazi. Kristina introduced Sol to her parents and occasionally took him home to dinner. Sol liked Kristina but knew he couldn't get romantically involved; at that time only Jews were circumcised, and he couldn't risk revealing his Jewish identity.

Nevertheless, besides their friendship, Kristina helped Sol in one vital way. The Gestapo had issued an order that every non-Jew needed a Kennkarte, an internal passport authorized by the Gestapo. In order to get a Kennkarte, however, you had to have a birth certificate. Kristina went with Sol to the local priest to ask him to give Sol a birth certificate under his assumed name, Jan Jerzowski. The priest agreed, but on the bottom of the paper he put in tiny letters that the certificate had been issued on the basis of verbal testimony. Sol had enough nerve to walk into the Gestapo office with this certificate and ask them to issue him a passport, which they did.

In February 1943 the German Army suffered a major defeat at the hands of the Soviet Army in the Battle of Stalingrad. As the Soviets began their march westward, the Germans announced that the Polish construction crew, which had completed the bridge project, was to be relocated to the west near Warsaw. Sol decided it would be too risky to go with them since it was likely that everyone would be strip searched at the new location and he would be exposed as Jewish because of his circumcision. He had heard some of the other workers, who feared being sent to Germany to perform slave labor, talking about fleeing into the forest to join up with a group of anti-Nazi Polish partisans.

By now the area was populated with retreating German soldiers and a sense of chaos filled the air. Sol went to see Taduesz to say goodbye. Sol told him how grateful he was for what he had done for him, but that he could now handle things on his own. Taduesz wished him well and asked him to never reveal to anyone that he had helped him. Sol promised he would never put Taduesz in jeopardy.

Before leaving Sol purchased a .38 caliber handgun and a rifle from a Pole who had hidden his guns before the Germans could confiscate them. He met up with about 20 other Polish workers near the bridge in Niźniów. Most had firearms and some even had grenades. They headed into the forest to find the larger group of resisters.

◆ ◆ ◆

Sol and his comrades had learned that the Polish partisans deployed lookouts to patrol the area. About 3 kilometers into the forest, they came upon the patrolmen.[2] Two of the men, who were about Sol's age, escorted Sol's group to meet with their commander. They walked deeper into the forest and arrived at an area that had caves dug into the ground. The commander, hoping to recruit as many reliable people as possible, welcomed them into the group, which consisted mostly of men but some women; there were no older people or children.

Historical data indicate that about 25,000 Poles in the General Government took part in the partisan movement, among them about 2,000 Jews, who joined both Jewish and non-Jewish groups.[3] Sol's group, which had about 100 people when he first arrived but later doubled in size, was a non-Jewish group, and an anti-Semitic one at that. The men often talked about the Jews—that the one good thing Hitler was doing was killing the Jews. Thus Sol never told them he was Jewish because he was fearful of what they would do to him. When the men went to the river to wash up, Sol never took off his shorts.

The partisans made their own homemade vodka. To Sol, who didn't like to drink and couldn't hold his liquor, it smelled really bad. But the men drank it like water. They expected Sol to drink too; if he refused, they would likely suspect something was wrong. So Sol forced himself to swallow whole glasses of vodka, which tasted horrible, and then snuck out to the side, stuck his fingers in his month, and threw it up.

Most of the Poles in Sol's group came from the region and had parents or other relatives in the area. The Polish population supported them with food, but the majority of people were pro-German Ukrainians who were hostile to anti-Nazi resisters. Nonetheless, Sol's group, which would go into the villages at nightfall, forced them to turn over food or simply took it if the people were uncooperative.

Sol's partisan group did not have any experienced military officers among them, and Sol said that they "thought more of survival than fighting." They were armed with guns they had acquired mostly from what the Poles had hidden before the war. Occasionally he accompanied them on small-group missions to attack German military installations or transports carrying supplies. During these times, Sol reminded himself of his father's warning: "Don't be a hero."

One of Sol's first missions involved placing a landmine under a dirt highway. The men dug a hole in the road, placed the mine inside, covered it with earth, and moved back into the forest to wait. Two hours later, they heard a loud explosion. They returned to the highway and saw that they had blown up a German supply truck. There were no survivors. They grabbed a few weapons and food that had survived the blast and retreated into the forest.

Over the next 14 months, Sol went on a number of these missions. Usually the men would plant the landmines on highways or railroad tracks at night. If there were a lot of Germans alive after an explosion, they would not bring back supplies. If only a few Germans remained alive, they would shoot them to get the supplies.

Sol was not privy to the inner circle of his group's leadership, but in the summer of 1943 he was chosen for a mission to

Stanisławów because he knew how to speak German. The leadership had learned that a number of SS had recently arrived in Stanisławów, and they wanted to know what was going on. They gave Sol a counterfeit document on a little piece of paper that said he had been called to the Labor Department to report for work in Germany. He was to meet a man disguised as a beggar who would be sitting near the train station exit. Sol was to say, "Hitler has a nice day today," and the man was to reply, "I agree with that completely."

Sol took a train to Stanisławów, and when they pulled into the station he noticed that both sides of the railroad tracks were surrounded by German police. A voice blared out through a bullhorn instructing everyone to first remain on the train and then come out through one of the exits. Sol feared that this was the end for him, but he didn't try to hide. He went forward right away and was among the first to get off the train.

Sol walked through the middle of the German police who were standing on both sides of the aisle that had been formed. He came to the front of a door, the exit to the station, where a uniformed Gestapo officer and a Ukrainian police officer who spoke Polish were standing. The Gestapo officer asked him, in German, "Where are you going?" Sol showed him his forged document and the internal passport he had from Niźniów, looked him straight in the eye and said, in Polish, "I don't understand German." The Gestapo officer said, "What did you come here for?" Sol repeated, "I don't understand." Then the Ukrainian officer began translating in Polish, and Sol told him he had an order from the Labor Department. The Gestapo officer took the document and looked it over, staring closely at Sol. Sol looked back at him straight in the eyes, shaking in his boots, and the officer said, "Forward."

Sol walked out of the train station and saw the beggar. They exchanged passwords and the man told him that the recent influx of SS was due to the increased security that was needed because of a meeting of high-ranking German officers. Apparently the meeting concerned possible unrest from the Ukrainians. Although the Ukrainians had collaborated with the Germans up to that point in the war, they wanted their independence. When they saw this was not part of the bargain, some began making plans to revolt. Sol also learned that the officers were preparing the German Army to retreat because of the advancing Soviet Army.

◆ ◆ ◆

By April 1944 the Soviets had advanced to the point that the partisans began making plans to disband. The Germans had already begun to retreat and the partisans who lived in the area planned to return to their homes. Sol did not yet know what he would do.

Before disbanding, the partisans sent a group that included Sol into Niźniów to secure as many supplies as they could before they could be confiscated by the Soviets. When they arrived they discovered that a regiment of Hungarian soldiers, who were allied with Germany and under German command, were controlling the area.[4] The partisans thought the Hungarians would not bother them, but they were wrong. The Hungarians rounded up Sol's group and marched them to a prison that was under the guard of two Germans. The Germans locked them in a cell and told them they would be executed soon. But in the middle of the night, a group of Hungarian soldiers arrived, killed the German guards, and liberated the Poles. Apparently they were concerned that if the Germans executed the men, they would be blamed and suffer some consequences.

An hour later, the Soviet Army arrived. The Hungarians forthrightly threw down their weapons and marched voluntarily into the prison that was now controlled by the Soviets. Most of

Children, Save Yourselves!

the partisans were local and went home. Sol still did not know what he was going to do and spent the first night sleeping on the street. The next day he decided to follow the Soviet soldiers as they went around the town ordering the residents to give them food. The soldiers did not mind Sol hanging around as long as he was unarmed.

About a week later the Germans launched a counteroffensive that forced the Soviet troops in Niźniów to retreat eastward. Sol went with them. During this time they were bombed and machine-gunned by diving German planes. Sol remembers lying in a field that was barren from the winter with his face and hands dug into the ground as bombs, bullets, and shrapnel flew all around! Dead people were scattered throughout the field. He laid there for half an hour. Miraculously he wasn't hit. Not even a scratch.

The Soviets continued retreating across the Prut River to the city of Chernivtsi, where they had established a larger base of operation. For the next two weeks Sol found a place to stay in houses or on the street among other partisans and civilians who were being drafted into the Soviet Army. One day a Soviet soldier grabbed Sol off the street and escorted him to the draft board. Sol completed a form in the name of Jan Jerzowski, indicating he was a Catholic Pole who spoke Polish, German, and some Russian, which had improved through the tutelage of some of his partisan comrades.

The draft board official reviewed the form and filled out additional military papers. He handed Sol a document with the name Ivan Marianowicz Jerzowski, and told him he would start training immediately. Sol reported to the military barracks where he was assigned a bed and locker and issued a uniform.

Sol's platoon consisted of about 150 men of Polish, Ukrainian, Romanian, and Russian descent who were placed under the command of a Soviet officer. The first morning they received instruction on handling arms and were required to march around in formation; and in the afternoon they received instruction in Russian. After about two weeks Sol was assigned to guard duty, a task he fulfilled for the next three months. Like the Polish partisans, the Soviet soldiers drank a lot of vodka. Sol started carrying a bottle to fit in with the rest of the men; he drank a little but did not like it. He also talked a lot with other Russians to hone his language skills.

By mid-July they began hearing loud artillery fire. At times the constant barrage of bombs was deafening. Sol's platoon was ordered to get ready to march to join other men at the front lines, where Sol felt he would likely be killed. Instead he came up with a plan to avoid this fate. He went over to the prisoner-of-war camp where German soldiers were interned. He snuck into a cell and took a gold watch from an unconscious prisoner. He was happy to see it was a Tissot, because he had learned that Russians especially loved Swiss watches.

Sol put the watch on his wrist and walked over to the Soviet command center. The commanding officer, a man in his sixties, sat alone in the office. Sol showed him the Tissot and asked, in Russian, "Do you like my watch?"

"Of course I like your watch," the officer replied. "Let's make a deal," Sol said. "I stay away from the front lines and you take my watch."

The officer asked to inspect the watch. He put it to his ear to make sure it worked. Satisfied, he said, "You are going to take a class to learn how to be a translator. When you come back, I will give you a commission as an officer. The two of us will be just fine."

Sol went back to his barracks to pick up his belongings and returned to the command center, where he was given a bed in the officers' barracks. The next day he began training as an interrogation translator and supply officer. The training was conducted by an officer of the NKVD, the People's Commissariat of Internal Affairs, which was a branch of the Soviet secret police. Sol attended classes daily for about four weeks and was indoctrinated into communism. When he completed the classes, he received the rank of lieutenant and was issued a new uniform and a black cap with a big red star. Sol tailored the uniform so that it fit perfectly. All of this time no one ever knew he was Jewish.

As the Soviet Army recovered and began advancing westward, Sol's unit remained about 50 to 70 kilometers behind the front lines, protecting him from the dangers of the battlefield. His brother Michael, however, was still in the Nazi concentration camp system; and it is to his experience in the camps that we now turn.

6

The Camps

The Nazi concentration camp system, which consisted of hundreds of camps across Europe, was used for a variety of functions: incarceration, forced labor, and extermination (and as assembly camps for eventual extermination elsewhere). Some camps, like the infamous one at Auschwitz, consisted of numerous subcamps. The system was run by the SS, and in 1942 the camps were incorporated into the SS's Economic and Administrative Main Office, the division that ran a vast array of SS business enterprises that relied on inmate slave labor. These businesses included companies involved in armaments, building materials, furniture, textiles, leather, fishing, shale oil, printing, foodstuffs, and mineral water.[1]

Initially the Nazis used the concentration camps to incarcerate their political adversaries in Germany (such as communists, socialists, trade unionists, and oppositional church leaders). Next they sent so-called antisocial elements (such as

Children, Save Yourselves!

vagrants, beggars, and convicted criminals). After the infamous Kristallnacht pogrom of 1938, the camps were increasingly used for incarcerating Jews, and once the Final Solution was underway in 1942, the extermination function of the camps became more central to their operation. Moderówka, the camp that Michael and Moses were sent to in September 1942, was still a work camp, which Michael said was "the easiest to bear" among all the camps he subsequently experienced.

◆ ◆ ◆

The Jewish barracks in Moderówka where the tailors worked and lived were separated from the rest of the camp in a compound surrounded with barbed wire and armed guards. There were about 30 tailors when Michael and Moses arrived, with two barracks for men, one barracks for women, and an additional barracks equipped with sewing machines and other tailoring equipment that had been confiscated from Jewish shops.

Michael said that the tailor-prisoners were allowed to wear civilian clothes and were given three meals a day, but the guards "occasionally took sport by slapping us around." One incident he remembered vividly involved the night a Nazi officer came into his barracks while they were sleeping and took one of the young men. Then he went to the women's barracks and took one of the women. The officer walked his captors to an empty barracks, where he ordered them to strip and engage in lewd sexual acts while he slashed them with a leather strap. After a while the officer sent them back to their barracks with a warning not to divulge what happened. They told the others anyway.

The most traumatic event that happened personally to Michael during this period of his confinement involved an interrogation he endured after receiving a letter from Sol. At the time, some of the prisoners were still able to receive mail from the outside because one of the barracks leaders had connections with the village postman. Previously Michael and his brothers had worked out a code so that they could communicate their whereabouts and circumstances. In this code they referred to locations or other situations by the names of people they knew. After Sol fled Krosno, he wrote Michael a letter to let him know that he was alive and to give him the general location of his whereabouts. After reading the letter, Michael destroyed it, but he remained worried that the Germans had already read it.

Two days later, Michael was picked up by two Gestapo officers who knew him and his brothers because the Bergers had done some tailoring for them in Krosno. They took him to a nearby concentration camp at Szebnie located about 3 kilometers away, where they interrogated him about where Sol was hiding. Michael admitted that he had received a letter from Sol, but said that Sol hadn't indicated where he was staying. The interrogators asked Michael where the letter had been postmarked, and he answered that he hadn't noticed. That reply earned Michael a good beating!

During the interrogation the Gestapo had a German Shepherd dog lying on the floor, and they occasionally urged him to growl at Michael with snarling teeth. After receiving another round of beating, Michael managed to convince them that he didn't know anything else. Obviously they had seen the letter and knew from where Sol had mailed it, but they hadn't been able to find him, because Sol had not mailed it from the city where he was staying.

After an hour of this ordeal, the officers called in a guard and told him to take Michael away, to where Michael did not know. He had visions of being driven into the forest to be shot, but instead he was taken back to Moderówka. Michael was happy to have heard from Sol, but he thought Sol shouldn't have written because it could have cost Michael his life.

♦ ♦ ♦

In August 1943 the Germans decided to close the Moderówka tailor shop and deport the remaining Jews to Szebnie. But Michael hoped for a reprieve for Moses and himself. The SS commander at Moderówka, who Michael said "was as greedy as the rest" and liked having his own personal tailors to make clothing that he shipped home to Germany for himself and his family, received permission from the Gestapo to keep 10 tailors in the camp. Michael's cousin, Felix Gebel, who had arrived at Moderówka after Michael, had been put in charge of the Jewish tailors. The commander allowed Felix to select the tailors who would stay. Michael assumed that Felix would select Moses and him, but to his great surprise, he did not.

When Michael first arrived at Szebnie, which eventually held about 10,000 prisoners, he worked a few days on and off in a tailor shop. But after that he mostly did makeshift work that had no particular purpose—digging ditches, then covering them back up.

Michael described Szebnie as his first experience of what a concentration camp was really like. The camp was completely enclosed, with towers manned by soldiers with machine guns and wire fences around the perimeter. The barracks were bare except for some wooden planks that were used for sleeping. Meals were served whenever the Germans felt like it—a small loaf of bread divided into 12 pieces, and sometimes a little watery soup. The soup was made from potatoes and turnips and occasionally some horse meat, which was extremely bitter, almost inedible. For the first time in his life, Michael knew what it meant to be hungry.

Although Szebnie had begun as a forced-labor camp, at this point it also was functioning as an extermination camp, or as an assembly camp that gathered Jews who were eventually shipped to Auschwitz. When the Germans liquidated a ghetto in the region, they brought Jews to Szebnie. When the camp got overcrowded, some prisoners were taken out of the camp and shot in the forest to make room for new arrivals. Then other prisoners were taken out to help bury the dead; these people were killed too.

It was at Szebnie that Michael also witnessed the way in which the Germans practiced collective punishment to keep desperate prisoners from rebelling or trying to escape. Occasionally a prisoner managed to escape on the way to the forest to be shot. When there was an escape, successful or not, the Germans executed 10 prisoners for each escapee. At these times, all the prisoners were assembled in a large field in the center of the camp, and an SS officer selected whomever he pleased at random. The 10 prisoners were then told to kneel, and the officer, who appeared to enjoy his work, machine-gunned them to death.

Michael recalled one time when the Germans built 10 crosses in the middle of the field. After all the prisoners were assembled, an SS officer picked out 10 men. Each one was strapped to a cross with his feet dangling above the ground. The rest of the prisoners had to stand at attention, watch the misery, and listen to the anguished cries. This lasted for hours, until all but one of them were dead. After the guards got tired, the camp commander announced through the loudspeaker that, because of his great compassion as a German officer, he would show mercy on the one living man. He ordered the rope holding the prisoner cut and then machine-gunned him to death.

For more minor infractions of camp rules, the SS would order 25 lashes. The guards placed the prisoner's head into a pillory-like contraption and begin beating him. The prisoner would have to count out the lashes, and if he lost count, the guards started over again. Most prisoners could not survive this type of brutality.

One morning Michael had no choice but to watch as Moses was taken away with a large group of prisoners. Michael assumed they were going to be shot. "That was the last I ever saw of him," Michael painfully recalled. "I didn't even have a chance to say goodbye."[2]

◆ ◆ ◆

In early November 1943, the remaining Jews were assembled and led out of the camp. German soldiers with rifles lined each side of the road, ready to shoot. The prisoners were ordered to run, certain they were being taken to the forest to be shot. Michael joined with the others in praying loudly and reciting, "Sh'ma Yisrael," "Oh hear me, God."

They arrived at a train depot where they saw huge piles of clothing. It was a cold, rainy day, but they were ordered to undress to their shorts. The captives were herded into standing-room-only cattle cars, and when the cars were filled, the guards locked the doors and the train departed.

The journey lasted about two days and not once were the doors opened. The prisoners were squeezed together so tightly that some suffocated to death. They were not given any food or water, and they had to urinate right where they were standing. They were not even given a bucket. Many perished before they reached their destination.[3] When the train finally came to a stop, the doors opened and they were ordered out. They had arrived at Auschwitz-Birkenau.

◆ ◆ ◆

The first Auschwitz camp, known as Auschwitz I, was a converted prewar compound that initially had been used to house seasonal migrant workers and later Polish military troops, and before expansion by the Nazis it consisted of 22 brick buildings. It was located just outside of the town of Oświęcim, renamed Auschwitz by the Germans, about 60 kilometers west of Kraków. The Nazis first conducted experimental gassings at the site on about 900 prisoners (mostly Soviet prisoners of war) in September 1941. They installed a gas chamber and crematorium, and used prussic acid (hydrogen cyanide), which had been used in the camps as a disinfectant and pesticide, for the gassings. They dropped crystalline pellets of the chemical called Zyklon B through small holes in the roof.

When SS chief Heinrich Himmler visited Auschwitz I in May 1941, he ordered the construction of a second camp, Auschwitz-Birkenau, outside the main camp to be used for prisoners of war. Construction at Birkenau, located about 2 kilometers away, began in October. By May 1942, however, the original mission changed as it began receiving prisoners of all stripes, including Jews. Gas chambers with large holding capacities were added, and special crematoria ovens with two to three muffles were built, enabling the killing and disposal of more bodies in less time.

Birkenau, also known as Auschwitz II, became the largest killing center in the entire Nazi concentration camp system, the symbol of the Holocaust. All told, researchers estimate that about 1.3 million people, most of whom were Jews, died in the gas chambers at Auschwitz.

◆ ◆ ◆

Upon their arrival at Birkenau, many prisoners did not comprehend the significance of the "selection" procedure they immediately faced. Others, like Michael, who had acquired more knowledge of the killing function of the camps, more readily realized what was happening. As Michael recalled, "We were surrounded by soldiers and ordered to line up in formation four deep.[4] Then the segregation or selection process began. Women and children were separated from the men. A couple officers went through the lines and pointed a finger at each prisoner, ordering 'Step left, step right, left, right.' I'm quite certain that the infamous Dr. Josef Mengele was one of them."[5]

Michael surmised that one group would probably be killed and the other group might be saved for slave labor. He closely observed which group appeared to have a better chance of survival and assumed that the group with the stronger and taller people would be picked for work and the group with the weaker people would be killed. Michael was standing next to a middle-aged man, whom he described as having "an obviously crippled leg." When this man was ordered to the left, and then Michael was too, he disobeyed the order and went to the right! The entire selection process, which took about an hour, occurred with such speed that the guards did not notice what Michael had done. Michael assumed that there were others who did the same thing, but he did not observe this himself. "You had to have nerve to do what I did," Michael said, "but I didn't hesitate. I could have been shot on the spot, but if I hadn't done what I did, I would have been killed anyway."

After the selection was completed and the two groups were separated, several trucks arrived and all the people standing in the group to Michael's left were ordered to board. Michael had a young friend, Herman Lipiner, whom he had met at Moderówka, who was on one of the trucks. When Herman realized he was in danger, he jumped down and ran over to Michael's group. Amazingly, no one saw him, but if he hadn't jumped he would have been killed along with the others who were subsequently taken away to their deaths. Later the surviving prisoners learned that those taken on the trucks were all gassed in fake shower rooms and incinerated in the crematoria.

Michael's group was ordered to march. He was barefooted and had only his shorts on. It was a very cold and rainy night, and he'd had nothing to eat or drink since leaving Szebnie. The new arrivals were marched into a large compound where showers were located and ordered to strip. Next their heads were shaved by camp workers and they were ordered into freezing cold showers.

After the showers, the prisoners were ordered to line up alphabetically for further processing. Michael and another friend from Moderówka, Joel Turek, tried not to be separated from each other. So Joel told the SS that his last name was Boigen, and he ended up next to Michael in line.

Each prisoner was registered and tattooed with a number on his left arm. Michael was given number 160914; Joel was given 160915. During the whole time they were incarcerated, the prisoners were called only by their number. As Michael said, "I no longer had a name. When number 160914 was called, I responded."

The new arrivals were issued a shirt, jacket, and pair of striped pants, all of thin material, which offered little protection from the wind and cold. They also were given a cap and uncomfortable wooden clogs for shoes. Then they were assigned to various barracks and indoctrinated into the prevailing rules of the camp. Finally, they were given a bowl of soup.

It did not take long for Michael, who had by now become an astute observer of camp procedures, to familiarize himself with the workings of Birkenau. The SS designated a chain of command and, unlike Szebnie, appointed prisoners to be in charge of the day-to-day operations. A prisoner known as the Lager Führer or Lagerältester (camp leader) was in charge of the entire camp. He appointed Blockälteste as block or barracks leaders, and Kapos as trustees or leaders of the work Kommandos.

There also were different types of inmates at Birkenau. Those with a criminal record were identified with green triangles of cloth sewn on the front of their uniforms. Those incarcerated for political crimes were identified with a red triangle. Jews, who were considered political prisoners, were identified with a red and yellow Jewish star. Although the majority of prisoners were Jews, there were many who were not.

The prisoners at Birkenau were housed in army-type barracks and made to sleep on bunk beds that consisted of bare wooden platforms with a little straw. The bunks were three high, with barely enough room to sit up. There were as many as 10 people sleeping on each platform, and Michael said they "felt like sardines." The Blockältester of each barracks chose two or three other prisoners to assist him. He had enormous power over the inmates of the barracks. He distributed the food rations and kept order. Rules were strict, and one was best to abide by them or he could be beaten to death.

Michael said that it did not take long for the prisoners to become aware of the gas chambers and crematoria, because of the smell and smoke from the tall chimneys in the camp. If one didn't realize this on their own, a veteran inmate or guard would occasionally say, "See that smoke up there? That's where you'll be going soon."

The crematoria were serviced by a special group of prisoners called Sonderkommandos, whose job was to sort the possessions of the dead and dispose of the bodies. Usable clothing and shoes were stockpiled in warehouses called Kanada and shipped to Germany.[6] Another group of camp workers pulled the gold tooth fillings from the mouths of the dead. Some of the gold was shipped directly to Germany, but much was diverted from shipment by the guards, who would have inmate craftsmen melt the gold and make pieces of jewelry. These valuable items were then sent home to their wives and families. According to Michael, "The camp guards and officers saw no reason not to enrich themselves, since there was plenty to go around and the Nazi leadership in Germany would not miss it as long as they did not know about it."

During Michael's time at Birkenau, there was a constant flow of new arrivals to the camp. The proportion of people who were designated for work as opposed to the gas chamber depended on the Nazis' need for forced labor and the room that was available in the barracks.

The daily routine began at 5:00 A.M., when a bell rang and all the prisoners were ordered out of the barracks. They were given 10 minutes to use the communal latrines and receive some coffee or ersatz (a coffee substitute) before assembling by the barracks for a roll call, or body count, which was supervised by an SS officer. After the body count, they were assigned to various work Kommandos inside the perimeter of the camp. Other survivor accounts indicate that some prisoners were taken outside of Birkenau to work, but Michael was not.

Michael did not perform any productive labor at Birkenau. Mostly he and his cohorts were given nonproductive assignments intended to inflict suffering, such as carrying stones from one side of the camp to the other, then reversing the procedure. They were supervised by SS guards armed with rifles and accompanied by German Shepherd dogs. At a command from the dog handler, the dogs would bite or just growl with snarling teeth to scare the prisoners. The guards often did this just for sport, which included beating prisoners with their rifles or wooden clubs.

The prisoners were forced to endure this type of work for hours at a time, and when the guards got tired, they would leave them standing in front of the barracks for the rest of the day.

Sometimes the prisoners were forced to remain in a crouched position for a lengthy period of time, which Michael said was "pure misery!" The prisoners did everything they could just to keep from freezing—exercising or just huddling together to benefit from each other's body heat.

Midday the prisoners were given some watery soup, but they were not allowed inside the barracks until after the evening body count, which occurred around 5:00 P.M. Following the count, they went inside the barracks and received a meager ration of soup. They may have received some bread too, but Michael doesn't remember this. By 9:00 P.M. the lights were turned out, and everyone had to be in their bunk. The next morning they went through the same routine again.

7

Auschwitz—Monowitz

Michael was fortunate to have spent only four weeks in Auschitz-Birkenau before being transferred to the Auschwitz subsidiary at Monowitz, also known as Auschwitz III. One morning at Birkenau, a selection took place after the body count. Hundreds of prisoners were taken out of the camp under armed guard and marched to the Monowitz camp about 8 kilometers away. It was Michael's good fortune to have been sent there, along with his friends Herman Lipiner and Joel Turek, because in the context of the camp system, Monowitz was a slave labor camp rather than an extermination camp per se.[1]

The Nazis had established the Monowitz camp in November 1942 as part of a large work complex adjacent to the camp that was operated by the I.G. Farben petrochemical corporation. The company had contracted with the SS to produce synthetic oil and rubber, and the camp was also called Buna, after the name of the synthetic rubber.[2]

Children, Save Yourselves!

It was at this time in his ordeal that Michael lost his two gold crowns. "When we arrived," he recalled, "they had us checked by inmates who were supposed to be dentists, but I don't think they were." It was these workers' job to remove all of the gold from the prisoners' mouths, as well as any bad teeth they had.

It immediately became clear to Michael that the conditions at Monowitz were better than at Birkenau. The barracks were neat and clean, and the bunk beds were covered with more straw, with only two prisoners assigned to each bunk. While some of the men looked emaciated, others looked well fed. Michael assumed that the latter were managing to get additional food rations. Indeed, those who received only the official meager rations were not likely to survive more than three months, especially if they had to perform hard physical labor. Michael began thinking that "survival was possible" at Monowitz, but that he would have to find out how some people were getting more resources.

A prisoner's position in the work structure of the camp was the most important factor in determining life chances at Monowitz, and survival depended on each person's ongoing appraisal about which work group was the most or least difficult to be in. Kommandos that did not require hard labor and that offered shelter from harsh weather were the most desirable.

I.G. Farben needed skilled laborers such as tool and die makers, carpenters, chemists, and the like, and they were willing to train some of the younger people for these positions. But Michael missed an early opportunity for an easier work assignment because of a painful sore he had on the insole of his foot from the constant rubbing of his shoes. After he was initially assigned to his barracks, he walked over to the camp hospital called the

Krankenbau, or Ka-Be, where an orderly applied some ointment and bandaged his foot.

Apparently at Monowitz the Nazis were willing to give workers some minimal medical care if it allowed them to return to work. In Michael's absence from the barracks, however, the Kapo had asked prisoners about the types of trades they were in and had begun assigning them to different Kommandos. By the time Michael returned, all the better assignments were taken, and he was placed in the category of a simple laborer. This also meant that he was separated from Joel, who was assigned for training in tool and die making, and from Herman, who was assigned to carpentry.

As for the general operation of the camp, the procedures at Monowitz were similar to Birkenau: waking at 5:00 A.M. and 10 minutes for using the latrine and getting a cup of coffee. Next the prisoners were assembled for a body count in the center of the camp on a large terrace called the Appellplatz, and then they were separated into different Kommandos and marched out of the camp through a gate that was topped by a large "Arbeit Macht Frei" sign, which translates as "Work Sets You Free." An orchestra consisting of inmate musicians played as the prisoners marched through the gates as if in a military parade. The Kapos saluted the SS guards, and the prisoners removed their caps to show their respect too.

Michael said that he was always alert to the different SS guards who were overseeing the men. "Would he take pleasure in abusing us, or would he leave us alone? We had nicknames for all of them, like Ivan the Terrible and Fritz the Butcher. But there were some who wouldn't bother you if you just did your work and stayed orderly. They had their own troubles and were worried about being sent to the Russian front and being killed or captured by the Soviets."

More important to the prisoners' daily survival, however,

was the Kapo who was in charge of the Kommando. He was responsible to the Germans for completing all designated work assignments and had the authority to administer punishment to those under his command. "It was important to have a good Kapo," Michael recalled. "A good Kapo would not hit you to show his authority unless he was being observed by the guards. Some Kapos managed to remain decent human beings and help others if they could. But a bad Kapo could be extremely brutal and sadistic. Often the SS chose people for these very characteristics. Many were murderers or other criminals under long-term sentences who were transferred from civilian prisons."

Kapos came from all nationalities and could be Gentiles or Jews. Michael noted that "there were even some Jews, who were decent people before the war, who became mean Kapos because the only way they knew how to survive was to identify with the system. Indeed, there were Jews in charge of us who used the same language on me and other Jews as the Germans, calling us 'Goddamn dirty Jews' and other such epithets. Some of these men had already been incarcerated for four or five years; and after surviving much brutality themselves, and finally arriving at a position of authority, they changed psychologically. To be sure, not everyone was like this, but many were. They would stand with the SS guards laughing as they watched the rest of us toiling at hard labor."

The first Kommando to which Michael was assigned at Monowitz was marched under armed guard through muddy terrain about a kilometer from the camp to a large area of completely deserted land. When they arrived, they began digging ditches, in preparation for what Michael did not know. They loaded lorries with dirt and pushed the cars on rails to another place to dump the dirt. The work was difficult, and it was cold and rainy. "We received many beatings," Michael said. "Our Kapos were merciless because they wanted to show the SS guards how tough they could be."

The prisoners would work until noon, when they got a half-hour break. They were allowed to sit in a little shack that had a wood-burning stove, which the guards sat around to warm themselves, and given some soup before returning to work. At about 4:00 P.M. they marched back to the camp, with the orchestra playing again as they walked through the gate, and as tired as they were, the prisoners had to march like soldiers. By 5:00 P.M. all the Kommandos were assembled for another body count. All accounted for, they were dismissed and returned to the barracks where each prisoner received a bowl of soup and about six ounces of bread. After a hard, long day of work, the food ration was hardly enough, and the men could never satisfy their hunger.

Every night after they ate, the prisoners were inspected for lice by one of the trustees in the barracks. If lice were found, they were sent to the public bathhouse where they were sprayed for what seemed like an interminable amount of time with a hose of freezing cold water. Twice Michael was sent to this bathhouse. Otherwise the prisoners were allowed to linger around the barracks until about 9:00 P.M., when the lights were turned off and they got into their bunks.

In his early days at Monowitz, Michael didn't have a steady Kommando and was repeatedly transferred from one to another. At first he did a lot of digging and learned how to throw dirt pretty far with a shovel. One time he was assigned to unload coal from a train. He recalled getting "black like a coal miner, and there was no way to wash myself clean." Eventually Michael was sent to the huge I.G. Farben complex, where he worked outdoors loading sacks of cement in a cement mixer that was operated by two other prisoners. The Kapo ordered the prisoners to form a single line of workers, and each had to pick up a sack. They were required to work fast, and if they did not, they would get kicked hard or beaten by the Kapo.

After a while Michael was reassigned to work on the manufacturing of the concrete blocks. This process involved assembling the forms in which the cement was poured. After the cement was poured and hardened, the forms were removed and the bricks loaded into lorries. When the lorries were fully loaded, three workers pushed them to another area for shipment.

Michael engaged in this type of work for several weeks, and he was getting hungrier and weaker by the day. He dreamed of getting an extra ration of food, but hadn't figured out how to get it. The prisoners who were able to acquire extra provisions were called "organizers." Those who were unable to organize continued to deteriorate, and those who lost a lot of weight and became emaciated were known as Muselmänner.[3] A Muselmänn's days were limited. He either died in the camp of malnutrition or beatings because he couldn't work, or he was sent back to Birkenau to be gassed after one of the periodic selections.

At great risk of getting caught and punished, there were many ways an enterprising or opportunistic prisoner could organize. Some were able to get extra rations by performing personal services, like tailoring for prominent inmates like Blockälteste, Kapos, or kitchen personnel. Some of the younger prisoners performed sexual favors. Michael never encountered any sexual advances himself, but it was known that many Blockälteste had their favorite boy, whom they sheltered, fed, and protected in exchange for sexual favors. This was true of Michael's friend Herman, who was two or three years younger than Michael.

At Monowitz, some of the non-Jewish Polish prisoners were in a better position to become organizers because they were allowed to receive food packages from relatives. And some of the prisoners, especially Kapos, were in a position to barter with the civilian workers who worked at the I.G. Farben plant. These civilians were interested in the various commodities that were stored in the warehouses but were not available on the open market. In return, the civilians gave inmates food—a loaf of bread, a half kilogram of salami or pork meat, or some butter. Since the inmate then had plenty to eat, he was no longer dependent on his camp rations and could give them to anyone he favored. A Kapo in this position could share the food with his favorite underlings. In this way a prisoner who was successful at organizing, or who established a good relationship with a Kapo or other organizer, could acquire enough food to sustain himself in good health, especially if he had an indoor work assignment. He was able to perform better at work and avoid life-threatening beatings.

In order to organize, therefore, a prisoner had to find a way to embed himself in the network of camp relationships that controlled access to additional resources. Up to this point, Michael had been unable to find a way to do this. "Whenever it was possible," he recalled, "we tried to form friendships to support and help each other. At the same time, we were reluctant to form attachments because we could be separated the next day. It was very traumatic to have a friend who was all of a sudden taken away."

At Monowitz, Michael only had brief contact with his friends Joel and Herman. They were in better Kommandos and had more opportunities to organize. Michael noted, however, that Joel never offered him any of the extra food he had. "I asked him for help," Michael said, "but he kept telling me he didn't have anything he could give me. Yet, I could see that neither he nor anyone else in his barracks were undernourished. Herman, on the other hand, did give me some food. In fact, he offered it to me; I didn't even have to ask. In addition to being the sexual partner of one of the influential Kapos in the camp, he was in one of the better Kommandos and thus had plenty of food at his disposal."[4]

One day, while Michael was working in the cement Kommando, a lorry rolled back and hit him on his right shin. Within minutes his leg swelled up to almost twice its size, and by the end of the day he could no longer walk. He was carried back to the camp by two other prisoners and admitted to the camp hospital.

The hospital was staffed with inmate doctors, nurses, and orderlies. The chief doctor was a non-Jewish Pole, but some of the others were Jews. The doctor performed an emergency procedure on Michael's leg. He gave Michael some chloroform to put him to sleep, and then made two incisions to drain out the puss to prevent the spread of infection. When Michael awoke, he found himself on a bunk, his leg bandaged, and in a lot of pain. On his fifth day in the hospital, a Polish orderly suggested that he ask to be discharged. The orderly hinted that the SS doctor inspected the hospital records, and when a patient was not discharged in a week and put back to work, he would send him to Birkenau to be gassed. Thus, Michael asked to be released and left the hospital with his leg wrapped in paper bandages. He was told to come back in the evenings after work to have the bandages changed.

Michael was reassigned to a different barracks and a different Kommando. The majority of prisoners in his new Kommando were non-Jewish Poles who were receiving food packages from relatives. Having extra food, their health was better than most of the Jews in the group, and they were able to perform better at work, which was still difficult. It was winter and very cold, and they worked outside all day. After several weeks, Michael began to look like a Musselmänn.

One Sunday morning there was a selection. All the prisoners stood naked, and an SS doctor, Hans König, inspected them. He picked out about a third of the men, and his assistant recorded their numbers on a list of those deemed unfit for work. Since the non-Jewish Poles looked relatively healthy, the ones who were selected were all Jews.

The following morning after the body count was conducted and the Kommandos were assembled, the numbers of the men chosen the previous day were called, and they were taken to a large holding room. Michael was among them! After several hundred of them were assembled, König came in for a second look and released a few back to the barracks. Michael realized, in his words, "that for me the end was near. I had no illusions about their promises of being sent to a resort camp to recuperate. There was nothing I could do but wait. Yet I hoped for a miracle, and indeed a miracle did happen."

As Michael was lingering near the entrance of the room, the doctor who had operated on his leg came in with his assistant, who was a Polish Jew. They spoke in Polish and Michael heard the doctor tell his assistant to pick out several younger people. Michael presented himself before them and asked for help. The assistant grabbed his arm, marked off his tattoo number, and sent him off to the barracks. He did the same for a few other younger prisoners. Later Michael learned what their motives were. Since they had patients in the hospital who were doomed because of age and bad health, they substituted the younger ones for these unfortunate patients, thus living up to an unwritten code of saving younger people who had a better chance of survival.

When Michael returned to the barracks, only the Blockältester was there since the other prisoners had not yet returned from work. He was a German Jew who greeted Michael with sarcasm, telling Michael he had only received a temporary reprieve and that he would be picked in the next selection.[5]

For the remainder of the day, Michael was thinking that he had to find a way to be assigned to a better Kommando, because he realized he had no chance of surviving if he had to continue under the same difficult work conditions. So he decided to go back to the hospital to see the Jewish assistant. Michael thanked him for saving his life, but told him it would be a useless gesture if he had to continue in the same Kommando. Michael pleaded with him to use his influence to arrange for a transfer to a better Kommando. The assistant gave Michael's request some thought and then wrote him a note to give to the Arbeitsdients, the chief inmate in charge of work assignments, who assigned Michael to Kommando 1 and to a change in barracks.

According to Michael, "Kommando 1 was the best in the camp. A prisoner had to be lucky to be in this Kommando, and when I marched out to work the next day, I was optimistic." The men were taken to a warehouse on the I.G. Farben complex, and for the first time in many months Michael was inside a heated building and safe from the outside elements. The warehouse was filled with all kinds of electrical supplies, and the Kapo assigned Michael to sort and clean light bulbs. The work was so easy and boring that Michael had trouble staying awake. Once the Kapo caught Michael dozing off, and he slapped him and gave him a warning to look busy.

The Kapo of Kommando 1 was a man from eastern Germany by the name of Hans, who spoke both German and Polish. He was a large, powerful man with a green triangle on his uniform. He had been a prisoner in Germany, where he had been serving a life sentence for murder. Michael said that he "had seen this Kapo enraged. He could beat a man half to death. So I was happy to get off easy."

In spite of his improved work conditions, however, Michael was still unable to organize, and he was constantly hungry. Then one day he noticed that Hans was missing a couple of buttons on his uniform. Michael told him he was a tailor by profession and offered to sew on new buttons for him. Hans gave him an inquisitive look and asked, "Do you know how to sew pants?" Michael replied, "Yes, if you can get me the materials."

By the next day Hans had already acquired several long striped overcoats of heavy winter material for Michael to use to make a pair of trousers. He gave Michael some needles, thread, a pair of scissors, and a thimble that someone in the machine shop had made from a half-inch pipe. There was a small room in the warehouse, a concrete bomb shelter that was off-limits to the other prisoners, which Hans designated to Michael as a workshop.

It took Michael about two weeks to finish the trousers, and Hans was pleased. He told Michael that from now on he would be his personal valet. Michael was to wash his laundry and iron his clothes. In return Michael would receive Hans's camp food rations, for he had no need for ordinary camp food. He assigned Michael to one of the first three bunks in the barracks, which were reserved for the elite prisoners. It even had a quilt. Hans issued Michael a new uniform and told him he had to keep himself neat and clean—wash his shirt every day (which Michael laid out to dry at night) and take daily showers in the communal washrooms with soap Hans provided.

Michael was now on his way to becoming an organizer, and he began to have hope. Receiving Hans's food rations in addition to his own, he started to gain weight and feel stronger. Three times a week he reported to the hospital to have his bandages changed, and although his leg was still painful, it began to heal. Every evening he showered with cold water because hot water was not available. It was freezing, but he forced himself to endure it. Previously Michael had not seen the point of showering without soap because he couldn't get himself clean, and in the winter he'd only risk getting pneumonia. But now as a privileged person in the camp, he began to think differently. A prisoner who looked dirty tended to receive more beatings, but if he made a better impression by keeping a clean appearance, an SS guard or another Kapo might think he was someone to respect, that he had some connections, and leave him alone.

Before long, Hans introduced Michael to the organizing scheme. Michael was assigned to put small electrical motors or other supplies into a wheelbarrow, cover it with trash, and dump it outside the warehouse in a designated place. From there another prisoner in Hans's Kommando loaded the motors and supplies onto a pickup truck driven by a civilian, who kept them for his personal use or, more likely, sold them on the black market to another civilian. On other occasions a civilian truck driver would come to the warehouse with a withdrawal order for certain supplies that were to be delivered to other Auschwitz subsidiaries. If the withdrawal order called for six electrical motors, for example, seven might be put on the truck. In return, the civilian gave the Kommando workers some food. Being a party to this scheme, Michael occasionally received some of this food. And when the next selection occurred and the SS doctor was picking out Muselmänner, Michael was bypassed. He was deemed fit to work and was no longer in danger of being sent to Birkenau to be gassed.

◆ ◆ ◆

Primo Levi, also a survivor of Monowitz, observed that various theories circulated in the camp as to whether to consume all of one's food at once or ration it over a period of time. The prevailing camp wisdom was that the former was the best course of action. According to Levi, "Bread eaten a little at a time is not wholly assimilated, ... bread which is turning stale soon loses its alimentary value, ... [and] one's stomach is the securest safe against thefts and extortions."[6]

Michael adhered to this philosophy as well. As he said, "Mostly I consumed all the food I had right on the spot. I never rationed my food because I felt that if I tried to save it, someone might steal it. Although there was an unwritten code against stealing from other prisoners, people would do it if given the chance. So I would just eat all that I had. I figured that even if I didn't get any more for another 24 hours, I was filled and not hungry."

Although Michael now had sufficient food, he was reluctant to give any away. He recalled only one instance in which he gave a Polish Jew some soup, bread, and tobacco. It might be tempting to be judgmental and ask why Michael was not more willing to share some of his provisions for the benefit of other prisoners in need. But although a prisoner was dependent on others for survival, it would be a mistake to assume that only acts of solidarity helped them stay alive. A prisoner who applied altruistic moral standards in an absolute way inevitably perished. Michael never stole anything from anyone else, but his decision to focus on his own basic needs was an important factor in his survival.[7] As he observed, "For the most part Auschwitz was a situation of 'every man for himself.' I thought about myself, not about other people's needs."

After Michael became an organizer, however, there were times when he did come to the aid of less influential prisoners. One instance occurred when Michael was sent out with some other prisoners to unload and move some heavy office furniture that was packed in crates. The assistant Kapo who was in charge of the group was a mean man, and he started abusing some of the younger men. He left Michael alone because he knew he was favored by Hans. But Michael finally got so angry with him that he interfered: "Why don't you leave these fellows alone?" Michael said. Upon that remark, the assistant Kapo raised his club at Michael, but Michael grabbed it out of his hand. As Michael recalled, "I obviously felt protected, otherwise I would never have done this." The assistant Kapo did not do anything to Michael at the time, but he reported Michael's transgression to Hans. Hans told Michael, "I can't allow you to challenge the man who is in charge. I'm letting you go this time, but I'm warning you not to do it again."

Although Michael's personal position was now fairly secure, his survival in Monowitz was by no means assured. A significant danger was diarrhea, which Michael described as "one of the biggest killers." Several times during his ordeal Michael contracted diarrhea—it was running down his legs—but he didn't get too sick and managed to get through it.

Prisoners also faced punishment for violations of camp rules. Any infraction of the rules resulted in a prisoner receiving 25 lashes on his buttocks in full view of the whole camp population. Occasionally the body count was not accurate, or some prisoners would collapse or die someplace on the camp premises. The Nazis conducted a search, and all of the prisoners had to stand for many hours at attention until they were found, no matter what the weather conditions were. All prisoners had to be accounted for before they were allowed back to the barracks.

Every once in a while there were escape attempts, but most of the escaped prisoners were caught. They were returned and sentenced to be hanged. At these times several scaffolds were erected on the Appellplatz after the body count, and everyone had to stand at attention and watch. One time Michael witnessed what he described as "the bravest act" he had seen, when several of the condemned men, who were members of the camp resistance movement, walked up the scaffold with their heads raised and proud expressions on their faces. When the SS officer pronounced their death sentence and the hangmen put the ropes around their necks, the men called out (in German) in clear, loud voices: "We are the last ones!" And just before they were all hanged, one of them yelled, "You are losing the war and will surely pay for what you've done!"

Michael said that the opportunities to escape or in other ways resist beyond becoming an organizer in Monowitz were quite limited. Because of the Nazi practice of collective punishment, many prisoners were not favorably inclined toward those who tried to escape, attack guards, set fire to buildings, or otherwise sabotage Nazi operations.[8] At the same time, Michael did sympathize with the more skilled and experienced inmates who were planning organized escapes or sabotage efforts that were more likely to succeed. But most of the men were not privy to these schemes, which were closely guarded secrets. As Michael said, "I was never in a position to join them, and I don't think I would have if I could, because I felt my chances of survival were greater if I didn't risk being executed for something I could choose to avoid. On the other hand, some prisoners may have felt they'd be killed anyway, which could have happened without notice at any time."

Michael recalled two or three times when the International Committee of the Red Cross visited Monowitz to inspect the camp, but these inspections were of no value to the prisoners. At those times the camp was cleaned up and made to look like a regular military camp. The men were given better food—a piece of cheese or salami, and even cigarettes were issued. But no one would tell the Red Cross representatives what was really going on for fear of what would happen after they left.

During the summer of 1944, after the tide of the war had turned against Germany, the western Allies (Great Britain and the United States) began bombing raids on the I.G. Farben plant. Destroying wartime production, not saving camp prisoners, was the reason for the raids. Michael recalled that British planes came during the day and the U.S. planes at night. After the first bombing, the men were immediately ordered to dig ditches around almost every building. Then, when the planes approached, an air alert sounded and as the sirens screamed, everyone, including the SS guards, jumped into the ditches. Michael recalled that "even without a direct hit, you could feel the earth shake, and we thought that the ground would collapse in on us. Some prisoners were killed during these raids, and I could have easily been killed too." Nevertheless, most of the prisoners approved of the bombings because they enjoyed seeing the guards frightened by the knowledge that for them, it was the beginning of the end. And for the prisoners, it was a sign of hope. As Michael said, "It gave me great pleasure to see the planes coming in! It gave me an extra psychological boost to get through the next day because I felt that every day I survived brought me closer to liberation."

8

The Death March

The prisoners at Auschwitz-Monowitz learned about the progress of the war and the Soviet Army's movements from Nazi guards and civilian contacts at the I.G. Farben plant. As Michael recalled, "We knew how far the Soviets had advanced on the eastern front. And this is what kept us alive, what gave us the will to hold on—the hope that we would be liberated by the Red Army."

By January 1945 the sound of Soviet artillery fire could be heard in the distance. The prisoners hoped they would soon be liberated, but the Germans were fearful about falling into Soviet hands and decided to retreat—with the prisoners, who were needed for slave labor in Germany. Everyone was ordered to assemble and prepare for evacuation, and they were told that those trying to hide would be shot on the spot. There was chaos in the camp. Michael didn't know at the time that the guards were in such a hurry to leave that they didn't search the camp for prisoners who did not report for the assembly. Instead, some prisoners hid out in the latrines or wherever they could. Michael thought about doing this too, but was afraid to take the risk of being discovered.

The evacuation occurred on January 18, and nine days later, the prisoners who remained at Auschwitz were liberated by the Soviets. All told, nearly a quarter of the 66,000 prisoners who were evacuated from Auschwitz lost their lives during the subsequent evacuation effort known as the Death March.[1] In retrospect, Michael regrets his decision to not hide, because the following months were the most difficult of his entire ordeal.

The Auschwitz evacuees were compelled to march for two days and nights to a camp in the city of Gliwice, about 60 kilometers away, stopping only when the guards wanted to rest.[2] The roads were covered with snow, and it was very cold. Guards were posted every 15 to 30 meters, and any prisoner who tripped or fell behind was immediately shot and left dead on the road. It took all of Michael's strength and determination to keep up. Most of the prisoners were wearing shoes with wooden soles. The snow stuck and piled up under these shoes; it was like walking on stilts, and every 15 meters or so they had to kick off the snow or they couldn't walk. At the time, Michael was fortunate to be one of the privileged men who were wearing leather shoes, which had been taken away from prisoners who had been gassed. The shoes were an unmatched pair of different sizes, but it did make walking easier. There was no food distributed, but Michael had a loaf of bread he had brought from Monowitz that he hid under his shirt and nibbled on throughout the march.

When they finally arrived at Gliwice, the exhausted men entered a camp hoping to get some food and rest. But the camp was already overcrowded, with little food available and only standing room in the barracks. Michael found shelter in a shed where some prisoners slept, huddled together for warmth. At daylight he awoke to find that many of them were dead; he didn't know whether they were dead before he arrived or if they had died during the night.

The next day the prisoners were assembled and marched to a train depot, where they were loaded onto open cattle cars. They were packed like sardines, and as the train left the station, snow was falling upon them. Michael found a spot near the side wall to stand, away from the center of the car. Those who dared to sit were promptly sat upon and suffocated to death. The dead were thrown overboard.

Although Michael had opportunities to attempt escape, he did not feel the risk was worth taking. Some prisoners took their chances and jumped overboard, but the guards shot at them from the train, killing most of them while the train kept moving. Michael's friend Herman urged him to jump with him, but Michael felt he wouldn't be able to make it. They said their goodbyes, and Herman jumped with several other men. Although it was night, the white snow made it look like daylight. The guards fired several shots at them, and at the time Michael did not know if Herman was hit. But in Munich after the war, he ran into Herman, who told him that a couple of the men who had jumped with him were killed, but that the others had escaped into the surrounding fields. They hid out for about a week until they were liberated by Soviet troops.[3]

◆ ◆ ◆

Meanwhile, the train continued west, and Michael lost track of time. He thinks it may have been five to seven days, with nothing to eat or drink except snow, before they arrived in Oranienburg, about 35 kilometers from Berlin, the capital of Germany. There had been a concentration camp in Oranienburg, one of the first of the Nazi camps, but that wasn't where Michael and the other prisoners were taken. Rather, they were ushered into a building with a large hall that held several hundred people, where they were given some soup and allowed to sleep on the straw that was spread out on the floor.

Coincidentally, Michael was elated to see Fred Seiden, one of his distant cousins from Poland. Fred told him that his wife and child had been killed by the Nazis before he'd been arrested and sent to a concentration camp. Michael and Fred were separated, but were reunited after the war.[4]

From Oranienburg the prisoners were loaded on a train and transported south about 450 kilometers to a concentration camp in Flossenbürg. The camp was located on high terrain surrounded by forests. It was very overcrowded with new arrivals from other camps that had been evacuated because of the advancing Soviet Army. They were a mixture of many nationalities who spoke a variety of languages: German, Polish, Russian, French, Greek, and others. The temperature was bitterly cold, and the prisoners were not allowed into the barracks until night. All day they were forced to stand around in the cold. The food rations were meager, and there was no work to be done except to sweep the compound or carry the dead bodies to the outdoor brick fireplaces. And there were many dead. One time Michael was grabbed by a Kapo who forced him to work several hours picking up dead bodies and shoving them into the oven.

One morning Michael woke and spotted some bread lying next to a Muselmänn. Michael shook him, discovered that he was dead, and hurriedly ate the bread. Normally, the prisoners were fed a bowl of soup and a slice of bread just once a day, but one day they were given the next day's rations in advance. Michael carried his rations to his barracks bunk, and suddenly a hand from the outside grabbed his bread through an open window. Michael put down the soup to chase the thief, who was a Russian prisoner. He didn't catch him, and when he returned to his bunk the soup was gone, stolen by another prisoner, and he had to go without food for the next two days. Nevertheless, Michael retained a starkly realistic appraisal of the man's dilemma. As he said, "In a way you can't blame these thieves. It was a matter of survival. People with a lot of scruples didn't make it. If you didn't look out for yourself, you didn't survive."

Michael remained in Flossenbürg for about five weeks, until he was rounded up with a group of prisoners and taken on a long march to another camp at Leonberg, which was about 320 kilometers to the southwest. The camp was guarded by Hungarian soldiers. The Hungarians knew that their German allies were losing the war, and their heart was not into guarding the prisoners. Everything was disorganized, and Michael was able to pick his own barracks and sleep wherever he wanted.

After about a week in the Leonberg camp, Michael was taken to a nearby underground airplane factory that consisted of a two-level tunnel dug deep into the mountains. The Allies dropped bombs in the area, but the tunnel was well protected. Michael was assigned the job of drilling and riveting airplane wings. The work was hard, but at least it was inside and out of the cold.

Michael remained in the factory for two to three weeks until the Germans decided to evacuate the plant as the British and French armies approached from the west. Michael knew that the war would end with a German defeat and that he only had to hold on for another month or two before he would be liberated.

The prisoners were marched from Leonburg to another nearby camp, but Michael could not recall its name. He had never seen a camp like this camp before. There were no barracks, only underground windowless rooms, which were lighted with electricity and dug deep into the ground. The camp was divided with a wire fence, and on the other side was a camp for women prisoners. Like the men, their heads were shaved, and they looked malnourished. Nonetheless, the men were happy to see that some women were still alive. They talked to the women through the fence, which was a pleasant novelty for the men, who hadn't spoken to any women for a long time.

By now it was spring and the weather was warming, but Michael and the other prisoners were again transported by train, this time to a camp at Mühldorf about 300 kilometers away. While Michael was interned at Mühldorf, he was taken to the nearby train depot to work. It was a busy station, and he worked on the docks loading and unloading coal. Several times Allied planes came and bombed the depot. During one of these raids, when prisoners were fixing the rails, the planes flew especially low and machine-gunned everything and everyone in sight. Michael dropped to the ground and saw bullets hitting the ground all around him! "I don't know how I managed not to get hit," he recalled. But luckily he wasn't hit, although others were, including guards and prisoners.

Michael was now more hopeful about being liberated by the Allies, but he also was dismayed at their disregard for the lives of the prisoners. As he said, "Although the Allied bombing put our lives in danger, I didn't mind since the aim was to destroy equipment that was important to the German war effort. But I really didn't understand the machine-gunning. This I found senseless. Didn't they realize that we were prisoners? It was clear that the Allies hadn't come to save our lives, and I could have gotten killed at the last minute for nothing."

Sometime toward the end of April the prisoners were put on another train, which had cars loaded with war equipment— artillery, guns, tanks, and other vehicles—attached between every second car of prisoners. They traveled for several days, not knowing their destination. Michael began to feel sick and feverish (later he was diagnosed with typhus). Suddenly another air raid occurred. The Allies bombed the train indiscriminately, destroying much of the equipment. Unfortunately, they also hit prisoner cars, and many were killed. But again, Michael didn't mind the bombing, because it was another sign that the Germans were losing the war.

During the raid the train stopped. The prisoners looked outside and saw no one around; all the guards had run for cover. Many prisoners deboarded the train and took off into a nearby village. Michael went with a few others to a home of a German family, asked for food, and were given some bread. The family gazed at the prisoners as if they had come from a different planet and appeared scared, expecting them to take revenge.

Michael rested for a while, thinking he was a free man. But after an hour, the German guards reappeared. With the help of some old farmers armed with shotguns and pistols, the guards rounded up the prisoners, returned them to the train, and forced them to remove the debris from the air raid. Afterwards the prisoners were ordered to board the train again.

Michael thought they were headed for the Tyrol Mountains, which run along the borders of western Austria and northern Italy, where they would have likely been killed. But suddenly the train stopped. Michael couldn't see anything, but he heard firing in the distance. The prisoners were afraid to move, and after several hours some German officials with Red Cross emblems appeared. The Nazi guards were gone, and the officers told them to be patient: the U.S. Army would be arriving soon!

It was nighttime, and the prisoners sat and waited. In the morning the first U.S. troops arrived. They distributed cans of food and told the men to wait for the second wave. Then the troops took off chasing the retreating Germans. A few hours later a platoon of American soldiers commanded by a captain arrived, bringing with them German Red Cross ambulances operated by captured German officers and soldiers. The U.S. captain ordered the Germans from the Red Cross to administer first aid to the prisoners.

Children, Save Yourselves!

♦ ♦ ♦

It was May of 1945. The place of Michael's liberation was Tutzing, in the southern German province of Bavaria. Nearby was a resort named Feldafing, which fronted a large lake with splendid villas on the shores. Feldafing had a hospital, and the villas had been occupied by German officers of high rank who were recuperating from war injuries.

The U.S. captain ordered the Germans to be evacuated from the hospital and villas, but all hospital personnel, including doctors, nurses, and orderlies were to remain. The captain put them in charge of the sick prisoners with a stern warning: "Should any of the men die because of your negligence, you will answer to me." The captain also made it known that he was a Jew from New York! That announcement made quite an impression on the liberated men, and on the Germans too, because they did not expect any sympathy from him.[5]

With several other young men, Michael moved into a villa that was furnished with comfortable beds. All of the survivors were served meals in a large communal kitchen that previously had been used by the Germans. The U.S. captain stationed American soldiers around the premises to protect them against any Germans who might try to harm them. Some of the healthier survivors, who Michael thought were Greek Jews, took off into the woods in pursuit of Nazi guards who had fled. Rumors circulated throughout Feldafing that they had caught several guards and killed them.

Michael's liberation by U.S. troops was quite clearly an auspicious turning point, even an ending, of his ordeal, but his survival still remained tenuous. The prisoners were not used to digesting normal food and many got sick. Michael had already been feeling feverish since the transport. He was taken to the hospital, where he was diagnosed with typhus.

For two weeks Michael ran a high temperature and was unconscious most of the time. When the fever broke, he found himself in a comfortable bed being taken care of by female German nurses. They told him that they had not expected him to live. But he did, and with good care he was on his way to making a full recovery.

A few weeks later he was discharged from the hospital. He was issued new civilian clothing and returned to the villa. Feeling much stronger, he sat around the lake, a free man, taking it all in.

9

Gusta

In March 1945, before Michael was liberated by the Americans, Sol left the Soviet Army to return to Krosno to search for survivors. When he arrived, he found about 25 to 30 Jews who had managed to survive by hiding one way or another. Some of them were not actually from Krosno, but from neighboring areas. None of his family was among them, and the family home had been leveled.

Sol went to see Taduesz and Maria Duchowski to thank them for helping him. When Sol knocked on the door, Taduesz opened it and gave Sol a puzzled look. "Is that you?" he asked. "You're wearing a Russian uniform? Did you have to become a Red?" Sol knew that Taduesz disliked the communists. "I had to in order to survive," he explained. "And still do."

It was a pleasant reunion, and the Duchowskis let him sleep in their home for two days because Sol was still apprehensive about revealing himself as a Jew to others. Later he went to see the Pole whom the Germans had put in charge of the family tailor shop before he had left Krosno. The Pole had acquired all the family's possessions. Sol asked if there were any photographs left, which the Pole had saved and returned to him.

While Sol was in Krosno, he learned of an organization called Brichah that was operating in Krosno. Brichah, or Beriha, means "flight" or "escape" in Hebrew, and the organization was established to help displaced European Jews try to immigrate illegally to Palestine, which was still controlled by the British.[1] The Soviet Union, which was tightening its control over Eastern Europe, officially prohibited the emigration but halfheartedly allowed it.

Two Brichah leaders from Vilna were stationed in Krosno. Being close to the border of southern Poland, Krosno was one of the last places that refugees passing into Czechoslovakia, Hungary, and Romania stopped. Groups of 10 to 15 Jews, mostly survivors of concentration camps, were given false identification papers before they left the country.

Sol met with the Brichah leaders, who asked him to help. Because of his Russian uniform, Sol could get around fairly easily. For about a month he traveled throughout Poland—to Warsaw, Lublin, and Kraków—leading small groups of concentration camp survivors to Krosno, where they were helped to cross the border into other countries and, hopefully, to Palestine.

On one of his trips to Kraków, Sol went to the headquarters of the Jewish Committee and spotted a beautiful woman. It was love at first sight. Her name was Gusta Friedman, and she had gone to the Jewish Committee to look for family survivors. Like Sol, Gusta had passed as a Catholic Pole during the war.

◆ ◆ ◆

Children, Save Yourselves!

Gusta was born in the town of Tarnopol in 1923. Her father was a supervisor on a farm outside of Tarnopol, where they lived, while her mother took care of the home. Gusta had three siblings: an older brother Benjamin, older sister Mina, and younger sister Dora. When she was 14 years old and finished with school, Gusta moved to the larger city of Łódź, where she lived with her aunt and uncle. When the war broke out in 1939, she took refuge in Tarnopol, which was on the Soviet side of the divide, where she lived with her grandfather and Mina.[2]

After the Nazis broke their treaty with the Soviet Union, the Germans reached Tarnopol and occupied the city. All of the Jews were forced to move into a ghetto and wear Jewish armbands. Every morning, Gusta and Mina were taken out of the ghetto to work, mostly folding bed sheets and blankets for the German soldiers. Every once in a while Gusta wrapped a blanket around her, covered it with her shirt, and snuck away. At great risk, she took off her armband, sold the blankets to local Poles, and used the money to buy food, which she smuggled back into the ghetto. As for the risk, Gusta said, "I was not afraid. If someone caught me, there was nothing I could do. You live or die, but not in fear."

After about six months living in the ghetto, Gusta and Mina were taken with some of the other young people to live in a work camp outside of the ghetto. Before they left, their grandfather told them they should try to run away in order to survive. Whenever she had the chance, Gusta snuck back into the ghetto to visit her grandfather and bring him food. After a few months, however, the ghetto was liquidated and all the older people, her grandfather included, were killed.

Gusta and Mina grieved deeply for the loss of their grandfather, but they also followed his advice. A German officer who was friendly to the young women told them about train transports carrying Russian and Polish women that would be stopping in Tarnopol. The women were on their way to Germany, where they would earn money by working on German farms. The officer advised Gusta and Mina to join them if they could. Otherwise they would soon be sent to a death camp.

Gusta and Mina, who had learned a little German and Russian in school, decided their chances of survival would be better if they separated because, as Gusta said, "If a Nazi ever hit my sister, I would have screamed and exposed us." Mina left first, boarding a train with Russian women. Two days later, Gusta boarded a train full of Poles. She did not have any identification papers and thought about what she would say if she was stopped. She decided to adopt a non-Jewish Polish name, Stanisława Urbańska, and tell any inquisitor that her baggage with all her papers had been stolen.

When the train reached the German border it stopped, and the passengers were ordered to deboard for an inspection by the Gestapo. Fearing she'd be detected, Gusta tried hiding in a small bathroom on the train. But two officers checked the bathroom and found her. One said to the other, "I bet you she is Jewish." The other responded, "No, she doesn't look Jewish. She looks German."

The officers escorted Gusta off the train and asked her to tell them her name. "Stanisława Urbańska," she replied. They informed her that she was not on their transport list and asked to see her papers. She told them that her luggage with her papers had been stolen. They asked if she was Jewish or had any connections to Jews, and she said no. Then the Gestapo put her under arrest and took her to a prison for political prisoners on the Polish side of the border near the city of Katowice. Fortunately they did not think she was Jewish.

When Gusta arrived at the prison, a guard ordered her to strip and take a shower for disinfection. Gusta had heard rumors about fake showers at death camps and feared for her life. She

Children, Save Yourselves!

told the guard that she was clean and didn't have lice, but then her fear subsided when she saw other Poles coming out of the shower alive.

After the shower Gusta was placed in a large cell with about 150 other women. The walls were made of stone and the floors were cold. The wooden bunk beds in the cell had no mattresses or blankets. Fortunately it was summer at the time.

The other prisoners, who were Catholic, prayed every day. As Sol had done when he had been imprisoned with Catholics, Gusta paid close attention to the rituals. During the day she was taken out of the cell to a launderette to wash, dry, and iron clothes and bed sheets for the German soldiers who were stationed in the area. The launderette was adjacent to an interrogation room, and Gusta could overhear Nazi interrogations of political prisoners. One of the torture methods they used to get people to talk was pulling their fingernails out with pliers. Gusta heard blood-curdling screams that sent chills down her spine!

While she was imprisoned, Gusta befriended another prisoner named Maria. Maria had a sister in Katowice who was taking care of Maria's infant child. Maria's sister had avoided imprisonment herself because her husband had joined the German Army.

Gusta was released from prison after being interned for about six months. Maria, who had been released a week earlier, invited her to stay with her family in Katowice. The family liked Gusta, but everyone thought she was Catholic, and all the time she lived with them she didn't dare tell them she was Jewish. Maria's sister's father-in-law, who liked Gusta so much that he wanted her to marry his other son, would curse about Jews when he was drunk.

Gusta remained with Maria's family until January 1945, when she told them she needed to leave to look for her family in Tarnopol. There was no transportation available, so Gusta hitched rides with Russian and Polish soldiers. When she arrived in Kraków, about 460 kilometers west of Tarnopol, it was night and pouring rain. The Polish officer with whom she was riding offered to let her spend the night in his home with him and his wife. Gusta accepted the offer and was welcomed by the wife, who immediately took to Gusta like a mother to a daughter. She gave Gusta her own room, clothes to wear, and plenty of food to eat.

The next day Gusta learned of the Jewish Committee that was helping people locate survivors. She went to the office, but they had no information about her family. However, they did tell her that they received new information every day. Gusta decided it would be best for her to remain in Kraków, rather than return to Tarnopol, and accepted the officer's wife's invitation to stay with them and work as a live-in maid. The officer was going to be temporarily stationed elsewhere, and the wife appreciated the company. But she did not know Gusta was Jewish.

One evening, a Polish professor came to visit the officer's wife for dinner and conversation. Gusta ate with them. When the professor commented, "Hitler deserves a statute for all the Jews he killed," Gusta was in shock as she observed the wife nodding in agreement. She wanted to scream "Go to hell," but instead said, "Do you know that in prison the Nazis used pliers to pull out the nails of Polish political prisoners? They screamed like you could not imagine. That you didn't see. That you didn't hear."

◆ ◆ ◆

When Sol first saw Gusta at the Jewish Committee office, he thought to himself, "I'm going to marry this girl." He made up his mind to leave the Soviet Army and travel with Gusta to Palestine. He approached her and asked if she'd like to have lunch with him. She told him that she didn't go out with Russians, so Sol told her he was Jewish. Still, Gusta wanted nothing to do with him for fear of blowing her cover.

After Gusta left the office, Sol asked the person in charge, a woman named Junka, for Gusta's address. Sol told Junka that he was a Polish Jew and explained how he had to join the Soviet Army to survive. Junka was reluctant to give Sol the address, but Sol persisted and she finally relented.

Later that evening Sol went to the house and knocked on the door. The officer's wife opened the door, and he asked for Miss Urbańska. The woman said that she wasn't home, but Sol didn't believe her. So he stuck his foot in the door, looked in, and saw Gusta standing in the room. Sol pushed himself in and asked the wife to leave the room. He told Gusta that he had made up his mind to leave Poland and try to get into Palestine where he could live freely as a Jew. He would be leading a group of Jews out of the country in a day or two, and since she didn't know anyone who had survived, he hoped she would go with him.[3] Sol realized that Gusta was afraid, but he promised to take care of her. If she wanted to go, she would need to meet him at the Jewish Committee at 10:00 A.M. the next day to make preparations. That is all he said, and he left as abruptly as he had come in.

At the time, Gusta would have preferred to remain in Kraków to continue to look for her relatives. But with her Jewish identity now revealed to the officer's wife, and the wife furious that a Soviet officer had come into her home, Gusta felt she had no choice but to leave.

The next morning, to Sol's great delight, Gusta arrived at the Jewish Committee, where Junka made false identity papers for them as Greek survivors of the concentration camps. Junka told them it would be easier to book passage on a boat in Romania, where they would sail south on the Black Sea, if they pretended to be Greeks rather than Jews.[4] But she only taught Sol and Gusta two Greek words: "kalimera" for good morning, and "kalispera" for good afternoon or good evening.

Sol and Gusta walked together to the marketplace so Sol could purchase civilian clothes to replace his military uniform. They did not talk much because Gusta was angry with Sol. "You did a terrible thing last night," she told him. "I had no choice but to come here today."

Later that day, Sol and Gusta went to a Brichah safe house, where they met up with other survivors. They shared a room for the night with about 15 other Jews, but there were many others staying in the house as well.

At about noon the next day, a Brichah representative took Sol, Gusta, and about a dozen other Jews to the Kraków railroad station. The train upon which they would be traveling consisted mostly of open-air freight and cattle cars, and all of the passenger cars were filled with Polish passengers. About half of them were still in their striped concentration camp uniforms. Still in his Soviet uniform and carrying a rifle, Sol enlisted the help of a few Soviet soldiers who opened the door to one of the passenger cars and ordered everyone out. After the car was emptied, Sol and his group boarded the train and departed. They made a brief stop in Krosno and then crossed the border into Czechoslovakia. Sol removed his Soviet uniform, threw it off the train, and put on the dark green suit he had bought in Kraków.

The train stopped for a brief time in Czechoslovakia, where local people brought the passengers food, water, and clothes for anyone still in their concentration camp uniforms. Then they departed for Hungary and arrived in the city of Debrecen. A Brichah representative led them to a school auditorium, where they rested for a few days, sleeping on the floor. They also were given food at a public kitchen.

On the morning of May 8, the survivors awoke to a big celebration, with cannons firing and music playing. Sol and Gusta went out into the streets to find people dancing, hollering, and singing. Germany had capitulated and the war in Europe was over!

The next day the survivors boarded a passenger train, for which they were not charged, and headed to Romania. They arrived in the city of Cluj, the old capital of Transylvania, on the Hungarian-Romanian border. Their journey from Kraków so far had covered about 600 kilometers.

Sol and Gusta's group were housed in a three-story community building, where they were provided with food and slept on straw sacks. They waited there for a ship that would take them about 675 kilometers further to Consanța on the Black Sea, from where they would sail south through various waterways to the Mediterranean Sea.

About a week later, a Brichah representative came to the community building and told the survivors that the British Navy had blocked all the ports on the Black Sea to prevent them from immigrating to Palestine. They would have to be rerouted by land to Italy instead. The survivors were issued forged International Committee of the Red Cross passports, which now said they were Italian, and waited for further instructions.

Upon realizing that it would be difficult to get into Palestine, Sol began thinking about immigrating to Los Angeles, where his three sisters (Frances, Eleanor, and Rose) were living, instead. He hoped Gusta would agree to go with him, and more than that, he hoped she would marry him. On May 17, on a picnic in a beautiful park by a little lake, Sol proposed to her while they sat on a blanket under a tree.

Gusta's first response was that he must be out of his mind. They didn't have a home. They didn't have any money. They didn't know where they'd be from one day to the next day. Gusta told Sol that she had grown fond of him, but that she wasn't ready for marriage. Sol told her he was deeply in love with her and wanted to start a new life and raise a family with her, and that he was a responsible, hard-working man capable of earning a good living. Gusta told Sol that it was too soon and that she wanted to wait. But he persisted, fearing that if they waited, she might meet someone else she liked better.

Gusta kept saying no, but she did not get up from the blanket. She thought to herself that she had nowhere else to go and perhaps Sol was the man she needed after all. Finally, she said yes.[5] They both stood up, hugged each other, and kissed for the first time.

Sol and Gusta decided to get married right away, because Brichah provided private sleeping quarters for married couples, while single people shared rooms. They went back to the community building, and Sol approached a man in his mid-thirties who was a rabbi. Sol asked the rabbi to marry them, and the rabbi in turn asked Sol if he had a ring. Sol did not, and the rabbi told him he could not perform the ceremony without one.

Sol told the rabbi that he would get a ring. He asked the other survivors if anyone had one he could borrow and found someone with a plain gold ring who acceded to his request. With ring in hand, Sol, Gusta, the rabbi, and two witnesses walked to the same tree in the park where Sol had proposed. The rabbi said a Hebrew prayer and told Sol to place the ring on Gusta's finger. In Hebrew, Sol repeated to Gusta what the rabbi said, which translates into English as, "Behold, you are consecrated to me with this ring according to the laws of Moses and Israel." The rabbi then said, "You are married. Kiss the bride," and Sol and Gusta kissed for the second time.

◆ ◆ ◆

The day after Sol and Gusta were married, a Brichah representative led them and their group of survivors to the Cluj train sta-

Children, Save Yourselves!

tion. They boarded a passenger train and traveled about 430 kilometers southwest to Belgrade, Yugoslavia,[6] where they were housed in a Jewish community center and provided with food and money. The initial plan was for the survivors to take a one-hour plane flight from Belgrade across the Adriatic Sea to the port city of Bari in southern Italy, but the flights had been discontinued. Instead, after two to three weeks in Belgrade, they took a train about 390 kilometers northwest to Zagreb,[7] where they changed trains, crossed the Yugoslavian border into Italy around the northern tip of the Adriatic, and stopped in the city of Udine about 280 kilometers away.

At the Udine station, the Jewish Brigade, a military formation of the British Army, registered the survivors, gave them food, and provided clothes for anyone who needed them.[8] Afterwards they put the survivors onto trucks that drove them about 270 kilometers south to Bologna and then by train another 680 kilometers to Bari on the southwestern coast of the Adriatic. Finally, from Bari they were driven about 180 kilometers further to a displaced persons camp at the small fishing village of Santa Maria di Bagni.

By the summer of 1945 there were about 15,000 Jews in displaced person camps throughout Italy. Santa Maria di Bagni was the largest; by early 1946 it housed about 2,300 Jewish refugees.[9] The camp consisted of many villas that had been used as an Italian fascist resort. At first the survivors were placed in one large community building that they named La Chofesh (Chofesh means freedom in Hebrew). After a while, married couples like Sol and Gusta were allowed to stay in a villa where they could have their own room.

Santa Maria di Bagni was the administrative center for illegal Jewish immigration to Palestine. During Sol and Gusta's time in the camp, the Jews organized daily demonstrations in front of the British Consulate to urge the British to grant Jews an independent state. Sol was not privy to how the Jewish leadership made decisions about who would be selected for illegal immigration, but he believes that political affiliation was a significant factor. Left-wing Zionists were the dominant faction at Santa Maria di Bagni and in the Zionist movement overall, and those lacking a commitment to Zionism or those who identified with the right-wing of the movement were often disfavored by the Zionist leadership who made decisions about who would be selected to go.[10]

When Sol and Gusta arrived at the camp, the Jewish Brigade had asked them to register and indicate their previous Zionist affiliations. Sol registered his affiliation as Betar, a right-wing organization. At the time, Sol would have been willing to go to Palestine before trying to get into the United States, but the preference for left-wing Zionists made him doubtful that he and Gusta would be chosen.

10

Living in Limbo

As one can imagine, the transition to a normal life was very difficult for the Jews and others who were uprooted by the war. Both Michael and Sol were fortunate to live in displaced persons (DP) camps of relatively good condition, because most of the Jews, according to historian Hagit Lavsky, were forced to "live behind barbed wire in ... severely overcrowded former labor or concentration camps. ... They were guarded and ... exposed to humiliating treatment and, at times, to anti-Semitic attacks. Nutrition, sanitary conditions, and accommodations in the camps were [often] poor."[1]

Help from family and new friends was also important in making the transition to postwar normality relatively easier. Michael and Sol had been in contact with their oldest sister Frances through the International Committee of the Red Cross. Frances was living in Los Angeles, California, with her husband, William (Willie) Schneider. It was through Frances that Michael and Sol learned of each other's survival and whereabouts. Sol received the good news through a letter, but Michael had it delivered to him in person.

◆ ◆ ◆

One beautiful summer morning, while Michael was sitting by the lake at Feldafing, his roommate from the villa came looking for him. An American soldier was asking to see him, he said. Michael ran back to the villa and found a soldier behind the wheel and a corporal sitting next to him in a jeep. The corporal introduced himself as Bernard Fabian from Chicago, whom Michael recognized as his first cousin, the son of his mother's brother, Hersch Leib. Bernard had immigrated to the United States from Krosno when he was 10 years old and Michael was 5, and he was still able to converse in Polish. Bernard told him that Frances had written to several cousins from New York and Chicago who were serving in the occupying U.S. Armed Forces in Germany, and Bernard was the first to receive the information.

Bernard was stationed in the Ulm region of southern Germany, about 160 to 170 kilometers from Feldafing. On his first Sunday off, Bernard took a jeep and a driver to Feldafing. He told Michael that Frances had written that Sol was alive and had contacted her from Italy. As Michael recalled, "That was the best of news!"

After talking for several hours, Bernard said he had to return to his unit, because he only had a one-day pass. But Michael couldn't let it go at that and asked if he could go with him. Bernard talked it over with his driver and finally said, "Go and get your things. You're coming with me." Michael replied, "What you see is what I got," and he climbed into the jeep and off they went.

They traveled on the autobahn and arrived at the base where Bernard's division was stationed. Bernard had a brief conversation with the guards at the entrance, and they were passed on. They went straight to a bungalow where Bernard lived with several of his soldier friends, who gave Michael an enthusiastic welcome. Michael couldn't converse with them in English, but Bernard interpreted for him. The soldiers nicknamed him "Polski."

In the morning Bernard went to see his captain and explained that Michael was his cousin who had survived the concentration camps. The captain was very sympathetic and told Bernard to take Michael to the supply house to get him a uniform, because civilians were not officially allowed to stay with the troops. Michael was issued a complete uniform, including a helmet—everything but a firearm.

Michael's initial impression of the Americans was very positive, which contributed to his resolve to immigrate to the United States. He particularly remembered Bernard taking him to the mess hall for breakfast. Michael had some knowledge of what Polish, Russian, and German soldiers ate for breakfast, and compared to the Americans, he thought they ate like paupers. The Americans had eggs, bacon, hotcakes, and coffee. And they could eat all they wanted. "Now I definitely knew where I wanted to go," Michael recalled. "America!"

However, Michael did experience one disappointment that stuck out in his mind. When he entered the mess hall, he spotted an African-American soldier eating by himself in the kitchen, while all the white soldiers were eating in the main dining hall. Michael asked Bernard why the soldier was eating alone, and Bernard just said, "Don't ask any questions." Later Bernard told him that the black soldier didn't belong to this division but only delivered provisions from the outside. Besides, he explained, the U.S. Armed Forces were segregated. This was a great disappointment to Michael, because he had always thought of the United States as the land of opportunity where everyone was treated equally.

Michael stayed with Bernard for about four weeks and began to pick up a little English. When Bernard was ordered back to the United States after completing his tour of duty, Michael was allowed to stay until the whole division left a few weeks later.

Now on his own, alone in Germany, Michael returned to Feldafing, where he learned that another cousin had been looking for him. He was Captain Bernard Buchwald, a successful attorney from New York and the son of his mother's sister, Yetta. Bernard hadn't left an address but only a message that Michael could find him in the military government in Augsburg, which was about 80 kilometers from Munich.

Michael went to Augsburg only to find that Bernard had already returned to New York, but he had left an envelope for Michael with one of his friends. In the envelope Michael found an affidavit from Frances, which indicated that she would guarantee financial support, as well as travel fare, if he was granted a visa to come to the United States. Frances said to take the papers to the U.S. Consulate in Munich and register for immigration.

Michael went to the Consulate and was told that he would be notified sometime in the next year when his visa would be issued and transportation would be available to travel to the United States. In the meantime, he contacted a Jewish organization in Munich that was keeping track of survivors living in Germany. He learned that his cousin Fred Seiden, whom he had met in the Oranienburg camp, was living in a little town called Trostberg about 90 kilometers away. He went to see Fred and stayed there his remaining months in Germany.

Fred and five other prisoners had come to Trostberg after escaping the Death March. They were aided there by a young German woman named Maria and her family, who hid them out for about a week until the American troops arrived. Fred had lost his family and was quite ill at the time of his liberation. Maria nursed him back to good health. The two of them fell in love and eventually married and immigrated to the United States.

During the war Maria had been harassed by people in her town for fraternizing with foreign civilian workers. At one time she was almost arrested by the Nazis for her association with a Frenchman. While Michael was staying in Trostberg, both Fred and Maria were beaten up by some local townspeople who resented German women who associated with foreigners. Fred was hurt so badly that he almost died. He was in the hospital for almost two weeks but eventually recovered.

For the most part, however, Michael found the German population friendly during his postwar time in Germany. All the people claimed to be completely innocent and that they didn't know anything about the extermination camps; no one admitted to being a Nazi. In reality Michael thinks they were scared that the Jews would take revenge on them. Nonetheless, they were very friendly and helpful. Some German families even took in Jews as boarders.

Michael made friends with both Jews and Germans. He ate in restaurants and sat around in beer halls. Food was rationed to everyone at the time, but Jewish survivors were issued double the coupons that were given to Germans. Thus, they actually had more food than the rest of the population. There also was a thriving black market in Germany and a lot of jewelry in circulation. It was a natural thing for Michael to start trading, and he learned how to get American cigarettes, coffee, and chocolate bars.

Michael and his friends were especially fond of the German women. Because of their black market activities, the Jews had a lot to offer that the Germans didn't have. Whether or not it was genuine, the women seemed to like the Jewish men. So when Michael traveled around to different cities, he usually had a girlfriend who invited him into her home to stay with her family. At this point he began to lose any feeling of rage he might have harbored toward *all* Germans for what had happened during the war. He knew that if he had come across certain people, he would have killed them. But he didn't generalize this sentiment to those who weren't responsible.

One of the incidents Michael remembered best during this transitional period of his life involved a young German woman named Heidi. He met Heidi while she was traveling with a friend in Trostberg. One time he visited her in her hometown near Düsseldorf. They went to a dance together where a live orchestra was playing. While they were dancing, someone turned off the lights in the dance hall, and a group of German men in their twenties grabbed Heidi away from Michael. Michael fought back and was pushed up against a wall. He kept blindly hitting them and finally managed to get onto the podium with the orchestra and started yelling that they were going to be held responsible for their actions. Then the lights were turned back on and the orchestra players pulled the Germans away from Michael. Michael saw that the Germans were still holding Heidi and cutting off her hair with scissors. This practice also was done in France and Poland with women who fraternized with Germans during the war. It was like being a traitor. In Germany it was the same thing. They objected when foreigners associated with their German women.

Michael was angry. He knew of a garrison of Polish troops stationed nearby who were part of the occupying Allied powers. He went there and told the Poles what had happened. It made them angry too, and they asked Michael when the next dance was going to be held. The following Sunday he went to the dance, and when the Poles arrived, they disrupted the dance and beat up a lot of Germans. "It was my revenge," Michael said.

Michael finally received his U.S. visa in July 1946 and was told by the Consulate to report to Bremerhaven for emigration. He sailed on a converted U.S. troopship and arrived in New York in September.

◆ ◆ ◆

During this time, at Santa Maria di Bagni, Sol corresponded with Frances and learned of Michael's survival. She also sent Sol an affidavit of financial support that he could use to apply for immigration visas to the United States. Frances and his other sister, Eleanor, who also corresponded with Sol, sent him a $2 bill every month to help with expenses.

Meanwhile Gusta became pregnant, and Sol took a job at a canteen near the beach to earn extra money to support his new family. He sold snacks like fruit and chocolate to the refugees who spent their leisure time on the shore of the Adriatic Sea.

One incident that stuck out in Sol's mind while he worked at the canteen was witnessing a large group of refugees surrounding a man on the beach. Keeping his distance, Sol learned that the man had been swimming in the sea, and when he lifted his arms, someone spotted an SS tattoo under his armpit. Apparently he had been an Italian member of the SS who was trying to hide among the Jewish survivors. The refugees pulled the man out of the water and literally beat him to death. By the time the Italian police showed up, everyone had dispersed and no one would tell them what had happened. Sol thought the SS man should have been arrested to face justice, but that it was wrong to kill him. However, he didn't want to get involved and said nothing.

On August 24, 1946, Gusta gave birth to a baby boy in an Italian hospital run by Jewish doctors who had survived and Catholic nun nurses. Sol and Gusta named the boy Jack, after Sol's father Jacob, and called him Jackie.

Soon thereafter the Italian government decided to disband the Santa Maria di Bagni camp and move all the refugees to a transit camp near Bari to the north. Then in October Sol learned of the day the U.S. Consulate was opening an office in

Naples, where Jews could register to obtain visas to immigrate to the United States. Sol, Gusta, and Jackie took a train to Naples, which was about 265 kilometers away, and waited in line all night in front of the office.

At about 9:00 A.M. a Consulate official opened the door and started the registration process. Sol and Gusta registered under their Polish names on a list of Polish émigrés. They were given numbers 182, 183, and 184. Since there were about 6,500 names on the list, they thought they had a good chance of receiving visas. Unfortunately, the Consulate told them they would have to be put on a waiting list because they were only issuing about 50 visas at that time.

Sol, Gusta, and Jackie returned to Bari, unable to immigrate to either the United States or Palestine. In the meantime, Sol took a job with the Organization for Rehabilitation through Training (ORT), a Jewish organization that provided vocational training in the DP camps, while Gusta took care of Jackie. He was paid $30 a month to teach tailoring to other Jewish survivors.

Through his work with ORT, Sol befriended a young Jewish woman from England who was serving as a welfare officer for the United Nations Relief Agency (UNRA), the primary coordinating and supervisory agency overseeing nongovernmental relief operations in the DP camps. The woman told Sol that if he and Gusta wanted to leave Italy, she could arrange to get them jobs in England through her brother-in-law. Her brother-in-law, whom Sol came to know as Mr. Maiman, had immigrated to England from Vienna in 1938 and become a successful businessman in the plastics manufacturing industry. Sol and Gusta decided to accept the offer.

The UNRA worker sent a letter to her brother-in-law, and within two weeks Sol received a letter from Mr. Maiman offering Gusta and him a position to work as a domestic couple (a maid and butler) in his home. With the letter in hand, Sol went to the Polish Consulate, where he was issued three new passports as Polish citizens; then he went to the English Consulate, where he was given a six-month domestic-resident visa for the entire family.

In reality, however, Mr. Maiman had no intention of allowing Sol and Gusta to live in his home or work for him as a domestic couple. But he did know a man, a Mr. Pinkin, who owned a tailor shop near Piccadilly Circus where he ordered his clothes and who was willing to hire Sol—not to work in his home but in his shop. The plan was for Sol and Mr. Maiman to go to the Labor Department, tell them that Mr. Maiman had been unable to wait for Sol and Gusta's arrival and had hired another couple, and get papers for Sol and Gusta to work for Mr. Pinkin as a domestic couple instead. As for where to live, Gusta's Aunt Toni, who also had fled Europe in 1938, had a small two-bedroom apartment where she lived with her husband, Leo; and Toni and Leo were willing to let Sol, Gusta, and Jackie stay with them until they found a place of their own.

With the money they had saved from Sol's work and the $2 bills sent by Frances and Eleanor, Sol purchased train tickets for the family and they traveled about 2,000 kilometers north to the French port city of Calais. From there they sailed across the English Channel to Dover, and then traveled by train another 120 kilometers to London. All told, Sol and Gusta had lived in limbo in Italy for about three years.

On the first weekend after arriving in London, Sol and the family traveled to the London suburb of Stratford to have lunch with Mr. Maiman and his wife. As they were about to leave, Mr. Maiman handed Sol an envelope, which contained 25 English pounds. Sol spoke emotionally about this gift of generosity: "Twenty-five pounds was a lot of money back then. It gave me a much needed beginning, a down payment on our new life."

The following Monday Mr. Maiman went with Sol to the tailor shop and introduced him to Mr. Pinkin. Mr. Pinkin agreed to hire Sol for 15 pounds a week. Next Sol and Mr. Maiman went to the Labor Department to change Sol and Gusta's official employer from Mr. Maiman to Mr. Pinkin—still as a domestic couple, not as a tailor.

Sol immediately began working in the shop along with 10 other employees. When Mr. Pinkin's fashionable clients came into the shop, they picked out materials, got measured in the fitting room, and then Sol and the other tailors made them custom-made garments. Sol worked six days a week, Sunday through Friday, while Gusta took care of Jackie.

During his time in Italy, Sol had begun to learn a little English, and in the London tailor shop he was immersed in an English-speaking environment. He listened to the radio all the time, paying particular attention to the pronunciation of words. Little by little he became able to communicate quite well.

After three to four weeks living with Toni and Leo, Sol and Gusta found a furnished apartment in a four-story building that they rented for 30 shillings a week. The residents paid for electricity by putting coins in a meter; when your time was up, you put in more coins or your electricity turned off. There was only one bathroom for all the residents in the building, and they had to go to a public bathhouse to bathe, putting coins in a meter to get hot water.

For the most part, Sol and Gusta began living a normal life. There was still food rationing, and they received only one or two eggs a week.[2] There was no beef, but rabbit meat was available. "We ate a lot of rabbits," Sol recalled. "They tasted like chicken."

While Sol was at work, Gusta and Jackie frequented the

local parks and gardens or attended nursery school, where Gusta volunteered in exchange for Jackie's schooling. On Saturdays the family would pack a picnic and enjoy the parks and gardens together.

After about six months, when their domestic-resident visas were about to expire, Sol was called to the police station and questioned about his living and work situation. He was fearful that the authorities had learned that he was in violation of the terms of his visa and would not grant him an extension. The officer who was reviewing his case looked at Sol's visa papers and said, "You're supposed to be a domestic resident couple. How come you don't live there?" Not telling him the true story, Sol explained that Mr. Pinkin had a small house and didn't mind if he lived elsewhere as long as he came to work every day. The officer asked Sol a few more questions, picked up the papers, and asked him to wait. When he returned, he handed Sol a stamped document that said "permanent residents of the United Kingdom." Sol recalled his elation: "No more restrictions. No more subterfuge. I could do what I wanted!"

Sol enjoyed his time living in England and thinks he would have been happy settling there permanently. "The English people were so polite," Sol remembered. "Everyone said please and thank you. When you asked someone a question, they would talk to you kindly." Sol also had gotten extra work doing tailoring on the side for another refugee, and he was doing quite well.

Gusta, on the other hand, was not happy in London. She didn't like the damp weather and the grime from the polluted air. When she hung out the laundry to dry, the clothes would get covered in soot. Sometimes she had to wash and scrub the clothes a second time.[3]

Nevertheless, within five years Sol, Gusta, and Jackie could have become citizens of Great Britain. But all of a sudden, in 1950, they received a letter from the U.S. Consulate that their registration number from Italy was under consideration for immigration and they should report to the Consulate office in London to receive their visas.

Sol called Mr. Maiman to thank him one last time for all of his help. Mr. Maiman tried to talk him out of leaving. He told Sol, "I've gotten to know you. You've got brains. You're willing to work hard. I came here from Vienna with nothing, and look at me now. If you become a citizen of Great Britain, you'll be rich, because the English don't want to work. They just want to eat fish and chips, and go to the horse races and football [soccer] games on weekends. By Monday they don't have a dime to their name. In America you'll be a peon, competing with everyone else for a living." Sol simply replied, "All my European family is gone. I have three sisters in America. I have a brother there who survived. I'm going to America."

After selling all the possessions they had accumulated up to that time, Sol bought three tickets on a luxury liner called the New Amsterdam and sailed to America. On the seventh day of their journey, in May 1950, Sol was standing on the deck as they approached the Statue of Liberty, impressed by its grandeur, fully cognizant of what it represented to the immigrant peoples of the world. "It was overwhelming," Sol recalled with emotion in his voice. "I was coming into a new country to start a new life. I didn't know what to expect. But I was fully confident that I was going to make it."

II

The Goldene Medina

The Statue of Liberty, standing tall in New York Harbor
since 1886, was at the time of the Holocaust an international symbol of freedom and hospitality for immigrants seeking a better life in the United States. A poem by Emma Lazurus
inscribed on a bronze plaque in the interior wall of the
monument reads:

> Give me your tired, your poor,
> Your huddled masses yearning to breathe free,
> The wretched refuse of your teeming shore.
> Send these, the homeless, the tempest-tost to me,
> I lift my lamp beside the golden door!

Prior to World War II, European Jews who aspired to
immigrate to the United States had referred to the country as the
Goldene Medina, the Golden State. The sentiment expressed in

Lazurus's poem, however, was not consistent with U.S. immigration policy.[1]

The first great era of Jewish immigration from Europe to the United States spanned a century from the 1820s to the early 1920s. In 1924, however, the National Origins Act (NOA) established limits on the number of people who would be allowed to emigrate in any given year from any given country. The quotas for different countries were set at a small percentage of those living in the United States but born in that foreign country in 1890. The year 1890 was chosen because it occurred prior to a large influx of eastern and southern Europeans (mainly Italians, Poles, and Russian Jews) and was designed to favor those of Anglo-Saxon descent. This policy reflected an approach advocated by anti-immigrant groups that wanted the government to preserve the racial and ethnic purity of the population. Thus Great Britain alone received 43 percent of the annual quota slots. Although the NOA did not formally target Jews, many of the bill's proponents proffered negative opinions about Jews in their effort to secure its passage.

In 1930, in the midst of the Great Depression, President Herbert Hoover issued an executive order to further restrict immigration by narrowly interpreting existing law that already denied visas to all persons who were "likely to become a public charge" (LPC), that is, who were unable to financially support themselves. Although the LPC stipulation was initially aimed at "persons who lacked physical or mental skills required for constructive employment," it was now construed to include "anyone unlikely to obtain a job under current market conditions." Thus throughout the 1930s and World War II, the annual immigration quota for the country was never filled beyond 54 percent, and this was not due to a lack of demand, especially from Jews.

After the war, immigration to the United States, as well as British-controlled Palestine, was still controversial. An immigrant needed to have an affidavit of financial support that guaranteed that he or she would not become a "public charge." But eventually, through the lobbying of Jewish-American organizations and with the support of President Harry Truman, quotas were relaxed. By the end of 1952, about 137,500 Jews had arrived, with more than 60 percent settling in the New York City area alone.[2]

◆ ◆ ◆

When Michael arrived in New York, he was one of about 19,500 Jews who were able to immigrate to the United States by the end of 1946. He was greeted by his cousin Bernard Buchwald, who took him to meet his Aunt Yetta (Bernard's mother). He also met his Aunt Hinda, his father's sister, and her husband, Chaim Hocheiser. Hinda and Chaim had a son, a lieutenant in the U.S. Air Force, who was killed in the war. Chaim told Michael that he had lost a son but had gained a nephew whom he would have expected to be dead. Otherwise, no one wanted to talk about what had happened during the war.

Michael's sister Eleanor drove to New York from Los Angeles, with her husband, Jack Weissbluth, and their 5-year-old daughter Sandy, to take Michael to the west coast. After about two weeks in New York, they stopped for a week to visit relatives in Chicago, where Michael met many members of the extended family, including Bernard Fabian. He arrived in Los Angeles in October and lived there the rest of his life.

It was not until May 1950 that Sol, Gusta (now using the name Gertrude, or Gert), and Jackie also arrived in New York. Like Michael, they visited with relatives in New York and Chicago. Sol went to see Bernard Buchwald on a day he was hosting a gathering of some of his successful attorney friends at his Park Avenue apartment. Sol recalled being upset when Bernard remarked to his friends: "This one is a little smarter than his brother. When his brother was here, I gave him an ice cream sandwich and he put it in his pocket."

Bernard, it appears, was one of those assimilated Jews who wanted to leave his ethnic culture behind, to show other Americans that he was part of the mainstream, not one of the marginalized who represented the ways of the Old World. According to sociologist Jeffrey Alexander, the "barely suppressed fear was ... that these raw and unpolished immigrants" (like Michael and Sol) would reignite public antipathy to Jews, undermining assimilated Jews' wish to be perceived as people of refinement and taste.[3]

Before boarding the train to Los Angeles from Chicago, a number of relatives came to the station to say goodbye and hand Sol some envelopes, which he put into his pocket. On the train he opened the envelopes and found a total of $30, which was a lot of money for an immigrant who had nothing at the time.

Waiting for Sol, Gertrude, and Jackie at the Union Station in Los Angeles were Frances and her husband, Willie, and Michael and his American-born wife, Mildred. Michael had met Mildred while working as a presser in Frances's and Willie's cleaning store. Mildred's maternal uncle, Paul Saks, worked there too, and it was he who introduced Michael to Mildred.[4] It was a moving reunion for them all! Out in the parking lot, 4-year-old Jackie saw that Michael was driving a beat-up Pontiac, and Frances and Willie a brand new Oldsmobile. Jackie looked at the two vehicles and said to his Uncle Michael, "This is your car? My daddy's going to have a nicer car."

One of the first things Michael told Sol was: "If they ask you anything about what happened in Europe, don't tell them. These people don't really want to listen. When I got here and told them how tough it was in the concentration camps, they said, 'Well, we know, we had a tough time here too.'" Nonethe-

Children, Save Yourselves!

less, the relatives were willing to offer assistance with housing accommodations and financial loans, which was no small matter in helping the brothers acclimate to their new lives.

It may be objectionable to Israeli Jews to say this, but in many respects it was the United States, not Israel, that was the proverbial "promised land" for many European Jews. Southern California in particular, with its warm climate and majestic palm trees, was an idyllic place to settle. Jews had first arrived in California, also called the Golden State, in the 1840s during the Gold Rush, and many of San Francisco's first families were Jews. But the postwar influx of Jews into California shifted Jewish influence to Los Angeles. Prior to World War II, Los Angeles ranked only seventh among U.S. cities in the number of Jewish residents. Within a decade after the war, the Jewish population in Los Angeles surpassed Chicago as the city with the second largest number of Jews. Only its east coast rival, New York City, had more.[5]

Although the residential concentration of Jews in particular districts of Los Angeles was not as great as in New York, more than one-third of Los Angeles Jews lived in areas of the city that had large numbers of Jewish residents. By the 1940s, the west-central district of Beverly Boulevard and Fairfax Avenue had become the primary axis of Jewish settlement in Los Angeles, but as this area deteriorated over the years, Los Angeles Jews moved further west (including to Beverly Hills), while younger couples purchased starter homes in the San Fernando Valley. By the mid-1950s, Michael and Mildred and Sol and Gertrude each had two children (I was born in 1951 and my brother, Jeff, in 1954; my cousin Jack was born in 1946 and cousin Marlene in 1951); and they had purchased homes in West Los Angeles with the help of loans from their sisters. Throughout that time much of their social life took place with other survivors. Families often met for picnics in the park. The children played together, and the adults rarely spoke of from whence they came. They were focused on the present, as Sol recalled, "How were we going to make money? How were we going to raise our children?"

◆ ◆ ◆

Even before World War II, Jewish immigrants to the United States often found work in the garment industry, or needle trades, and it was of course natural for Michael and Sol to seek employment in this area too.[6] Michael's primary job, until the mid-1950s, was at a Jewish-owned ladies garment factory in downtown Los Angeles, which employed mostly Mexican women workers. He became a union shop steward in the factory and got Sol a job there too. They worked as sewing machine operators, making entire coats, about 15 to 20 a day. The work was hard, but they were earning money, which they supplemented by making and selling clothes out of their homes on the weekends. For immigrants who came to the United States with nothing but family ties, they were doing quite well.

In 1955 the brothers decided to try to make a go of it on their own, and they purchased a tailor shop on Pico Boulevard, which they called S & M Tailors. But there wasn't enough business for both of them to earn a living, and Sol in particular wanted to get out of tailoring altogether. Eleanor and Jack had just sold their liquor store, and they encouraged Michael and Sol to buy one of their own. They offered to help them find a store, lend them some money, and teach them the business. Such assistance from family is characteristic of ethnic-based enterprises that have been a source of upward mobility for immigrants in the United States, and small retail outlets like liquor stores were a niche for immigrant Jews.[7]

Michael and Sol bought a store on Hoover Street near the Los Angeles Coliseum in an African-American neighborhood

Children, Save Yourselves!

in south-central Los Angeles. The store space itself was rented, but the license, merchandise, and general goodwill cost $30,000. Between the two of them, the brothers had accumulated about $15,000, most of which came from restitution money they had received from Germany; Eleanor and Jack lent them the rest.

The Hoover Street store was small, not large enough to yield a volume of sales that could support two families. However, the two adjacent stores were vacant, and they decided to rent all three, knock out the walls, and build one larger store. What was once a small liquor store became a small grocery and department store of sorts, selling everything from food to clothing, radios, and televisions. In addition to employing family members, the store hired several African Americans, most notably Spike Holbert, a tall, charismatic man who helped make Hoover Liquor, as it was called, an institution in the neighborhood. It offered check-cashing services, lines of no-interest credit, and generous Christmastime gifts to customers.

The work of running a store like this was difficult. Both brothers put in at least six days a week, typically at least 10 hours a day. But the business grew, and they prospered financially, enough to buy a second store a little further west on Santa Barbara Avenue. Then came the infamous Los Angeles Watts Riot of August 1965.

The riot was precipitated by conflict between the black community and the Los Angeles police, and the looting and property destruction that ensued had a particularly hard impact on Jewish merchants, who owned the majority of furniture stores, food shops, and liquor stores in the riot-torn area.[8] The rioting lasted for several days, and the National Guard was called in to help quell the unrest. Guard troops and the police blocked off entrance into the affected areas. News reports indicated that the Bergers' Santa Barbara store was outside of the prime riot area, but the Hoover store was in the middle of the fray. Nonetheless,

Michael and Sol wanted to go to the store to see if they still had a business and to protect anything that remained.

With a loaded shotgun and handgun in the trunk of their car, Michael and Sol headed east. When they reached La Brea Avenue, they came upon a police roadblock. A police officer asked them where they were going, and they explained that their business had been looted. The officer said it was too dangerous and they couldn't go any further. The brothers replied that they wanted to go anyway. The officer asked if they had any arms and if they were loaded. The brothers said yes. The officer asked, "Do you still want to go? I'm telling you not to go. It's too dangerous." They said yes. Finally the officer said, "Okay, then. But I'm warning you. If you get attacked, and if you take out your guns, you better use them. Otherwise, you'll be killed."

When Michael and Sol arrived at the store, they found Spike and his brother Bill, also an employee, standing guard, trying to deter further damage. They had been protecting the store, which was important to their livelihood, allowing looters to take what they wanted as long as they didn't set fire to the property. "All the windows were broken," Sol recalled. "No merchandise. Everything was taken."

The many neighbors who were loyal customers of Hoover Liquor had not been among the looters, and they wrote up a petition expressing their sincere apologies for what had happened. They asked residents to contribute 25 cents, 50 cents, whatever they could afford, to help open the store as soon as possible, because there weren't other places to shop nearby. Michael and Sol had insurance for the merchandise, but the claim wasn't settled right away; and there was no insurance for the building itself, as insurance companies redlined the area. They hired a handyman to board up the windows, ordered some merchandise from a wholesale house, and reopened the store.

Children, Save Yourselves!

In spite of the goodwill of many residents, there were others who were hostile, coming into the store and saying things like, "Whitey, if you stay here, I'm gonna burn you down." Sol, who was carrying his revolver on his belt, replied, "If you try to do anything, I'll blow your brains out." Thus, both brothers had had enough. They called in a real estate broker and told him they wanted to sell. The next day they sold the license to an African-American liquor salesman for $60,000, which was far less than it was worth before the rioting.

Spike, who preferred to work for the brothers rather than the new owner, went to the Santa Barbara store with them. This store, however, was small, and there was no space for expansion to build up the business. It also was an increasingly dangerous neighborhood, and they experienced a few hold-ups. Sol decided he wanted out and that it was time to end the partnership with Michael. He started looking for another store to buy and found one in the city of Burbank in the San Fernando Valley. When Michael first heard about this, his initial response was: "You want to leave me here?" Sol said, "Okay, you can take the Burbank store and I'll stay here." Thus, after working in the liquor business together for about 15 years, the brothers split up.

Upon his retirement from the liquor business, Sol sold the Santa Barbara store to Spike, helping him with the financing as well. Sol later attended community college where he obtained his real estate license and embarked on a successful "post-retirement" career as a Beverly Hills real estate broker. After Michael sold the Burbank store, he worked as a night manager in a liquor store and did freelance tailoring out of his home. Both brothers also owned and managed apartment buildings and spent a good deal of time managing their investments in the stock market.

In his study of postwar Jewish survivors in the United States, sociologist William Helmreich found that most fared quite well economically. To be sure, there were some who fared poorly, and Helmreich surmises that this was the result of "excessive caution, a reluctance to take chances."[9] But Michael and Sol were never averse to taking chances, and through all their trials and tribulations as immigrant businessmen, they were able to move into the American middle (if not upper-middle) class. They were able to buy comfortable homes in a relatively affluent area of West Los Angeles and send their children to college without having to take out loans, so that they, too, could settle into the middle class, and so on for the children of the next generation. This intergenerational progression was facilitated by the general postwar economic expansion and increased accessibility and affordability of higher education in the United States, which allowed Jews to move into the professional occupational class: Michael's and Sol's descendents joined the ranks of doctors, lawyers, computer technology specialists, university professors, teachers, and social workers.

Important as well to the intergenerational trajectory of the Berger family and other Jewish Americans was the general decline of the anti-Semitism that had marked the prewar period. Although at one time employers, institutions of higher education, and neighborhood covenants discriminated against Jews, in the latter half of the twentieth century, this was no longer the case. Jeffrey Alexander attributes this decline, in large part, to the cultural trauma of the Holocaust, as if Americans were saying, "This country is not like Germany." During the war, he observes, Americans' repulsion of Nazism had little explicit connection with the Jewish genocide, but after the war a different mentality took hold. Although the particularity of the Jewish tragedy was at first downplayed, it was not concealed, and good-willed Americans came to believe that being "against the

Nazis" meant "being with the Jews" and valuing the Jewish contribution to a common "Judeo-Christian" heritage.[10] Moreover, a large majority of non-Jewish Americans came to view Jews as a friendly, hard-working, and religious people.

It was in this context that Jewish Americans became one of the most economically successful immigrant groups in the country and among the most affluent Jews in the world. At the same time, rates of interfaith marriage rose, and involvement in organized Judaism declined, leading to a diminution of ethnic cohesion and group identity. In many respects, the state of Jewish ethnicity paralleled that of other white groups (such as the Irish, Italians, and Poles) who were historically treated as marginalized minorities by mainstream society and who self-identified as such, but for whom ethnicity has become a rather shallow and amorphous experience. Sociologist Herbert Gans calls this "symbolic ethnicity," an ethnicity tied more to nostalgic sentiments about family and family lineage than to active membership in a larger social network.[11]

Journalist Samuel Freedman is among those who believe that without a committed community of religious adherents, Jewish Americans as a distinct ethnic group will cease "to exist in any meaningful way."[12] In this regard, sociologists Seymour Martin Lipset and Earl Raab note that most Jewish Americans' knowledge of their religion is "thin at best and becoming thinner."[13] To be sure, some holidays such as Hanukkah and Passover continue to be observed by a large majority of Jews, but these commemorations are often viewed as opportunities to get together with family rather than as an expression of religious faith. And even these "practices can be expected to diminish as older generations disappear and as intermarriage rates increase even further."

Still, Lipset and Raab are impressed that even secular Jews who do not participate in organized religious activities often express an affinity for the cultural values and proscriptions for living that they associate with their Jewish heritage. They have multiple allegiances beyond the Jewish community and cherish the freedom they now have to choose their religious affiliation or disregard it as the case may be.

Children, Save Yourselves!

Epilogue

W illiam Helmreich observes that most of the difficulties encountered by Holocaust survivors in the United States fall "within the normal boundaries of the struggles common to all immigrants."[1] Indeed, the so-called "survivor syndrome" of psychopathology that has been a prominent feature of the psychiatric literature seems out of sync with the experiences of many survivors.[2] These characterizations were based on clinical samples and have not held up under the scrutiny of more carefully designed studies, which do not find survivors differing significantly from other groups in terms of symptoms of pathology.[3] Much of this viewpoint gained a foothold in the aftermath of the war, as survivors filing German indemnification claims for financial restitution had to demonstrate that they suffered from symptoms unrelated to their prewar personalities or experiences. Survivors, and those evaluating them, were forced to emphasize their disabilities and not their resilience and positive functioning.

To be sure survivors had nightmares, but they did not have difficulty reinvesting in life. They often threw themselves into their work, and were overprotective of and had high aspirations for their children, but this orientation to present concerns helped them move forward with their lives, especially in a social climate that discouraged them from talking about their experiences. Upon retirement, however, and with children grown and moved out of the home, the cessation of maximal activity often brought on a renewed challenge of memory. For some, as psychiatrist Shamai Davidson observed, there was "the increasing awareness that life is not forever, and that one must remember before one ends one's journey."[4] For others, their active lives had been a way of avoiding their pain and mourning for lost loved ones. Now the past began to reemerge, becoming "a resource or a menace" that was potentially debilitating but also potentially rehabilitating.[5]

Although many survivors chose to avoid embracing the past, others relished the opportunity afforded by the contemporary social receptivity to the "survivor," a status of respect now conferred on them that was in contradistinction to what they had experienced in the immediate postwar years. Moreover, as psychologist Boaz Kahana and colleagues observe, research on postwar adjustment of Holocaust survivors underscores "the potential value of sharing and disclosing traumatic experiences to willing and interested parties," especially family and friends; and those who were able to do so exhibited better mental health than those who were not.[6] For those who chose to break their silence, to speak about what they had concealed for so many years, the survivor role also provided a way for them to feel that they were educating the public about the need to prevent other genocides.

My father embraced this role. When I called him in November 1987 after hearing Robert Clary's lecture, he did not hesitate; he was ready to tell his story (see Prologue). Until he died of lung cancer in December 1994, he also gave numerous talks at middle schools, high schools, and colleges; and he became a docent at the Simon Wiesenthal Center's Museum of Tolerance, which was just around the corner from his home.

Soon after my father began telling me his story, he decided he wanted to make a trip to Poland, the first time he would return to his homeland since the war. In the spring of 1989, my mother, brother, two cousins, and I went with him. Before embarking on the pilgrimage, my father began reacquainting himself with the Polish language, which he hadn't spoken in four decades. He started by reading Polish newspapers and then by visiting regularly with a group of Poles he befriended at the LOT Polish airlines ticket office in Los Angeles.

During our time in Poland, we traveled to several cities and towns, including my father's hometown in Krosno, the mass grave site near the village of Barwinek where we believe my grandfather is buried,[7] several abandoned Jewish cemeteries, Auschwitz, and other Holocaust memorial sites. It was a moving experience that evoked sadness in all of us. But we were not morose, because the trip was also exhilarating for my father. I could see that he was actually having the time of his life. He talked fondly about his home, school, and places of recreation he had enjoyed as a youth. He loved to talk to people and struck up conversations (in Polish) with strangers everywhere we went. We also had a lovely visit with Taduesz and Maria Duchowski, the couple who had helped my uncle, and their son Henryk, who had remained in contact with my uncle over the years.

One evening during our trip, my father told me that he felt that his wartime experience seemed less for naught now that I was writing about it. This pleased me to no end to know that he thought the family project we had undertaken was important and beneficial to him. And when he walked through the gates of Auschwitz during our tour, he said that he felt as if he had triumphed over Hitler, because here he was still alive and well, while Hitler was long dead.

When we returned to Los Angeles, we were visited by Eddie Small, a family friend who also was a Holocaust survivor from Poland. Eddie told us, with some regret in his voice, that his son was not interested in hearing about his experience. He admitted, however, that he'd rather not talk about it himself. "The pain never goes away," he said. "I'd rather play cards and try to forget about it." To this my father replied, "It's good to talk about it, not to deny it, so you don't feel like it was a wasted experience."

When my father was dying of lung cancer, which took his life just six weeks after his diagnosis, we had a heartrending talk about a number of personal matters. He told me that he had been experiencing more nightmares about the past since he had assumed the "survivor" role. Remembering did have its costs, and he wondered whether it had been worth it. I assured him that it had, and I reminded him of all the appreciative letters he had received from students over the last few years (see Appendix). I'm not sure if he was convinced, but he seemed comforted by the thought.

My uncle was initially more reluctant than my father to embrace the role of the survivor. This stemmed, in part, from his belief that he was not an authentic representative of the survivor experience because he had not been in a concentration camp. But before my father died, he asked Sol to promise to take on the responsibility of telling our family's story. Sol promised him that he would, and indeed he did.

At the same time, I think that my father's and uncle's different modes of wartime survival left them with different attitudes toward Poland. Because he survived outside of the camps, my uncle was exposed even more than my father to the life-threatening actions of anti-Semitic Poles, and for six decades after

Children, Save Yourselves!

the war he had no desire to visit the country of his birth. But when he was recuperating from a serious hip injury in 2007, he decided he wanted to make a pilgrimage to his homeland one time before he died. He felt comfortable making the trip with his son, Jack, who was a medical doctor, and they planned the trip, including a visit to Israel, for the spring of 2008.

Coincidence would have it that a few weeks before their trip, I met a professor at the University of Northern Iowa, Stephen Gaies, who was taking a group of American students to Poland as part of a travel study course. They would be in Poland the same time as my uncle. Moreover, Stephen had a colleague, Wladek Witalisz, who was not only a professor at Jagiellonian University in Kraków, but the Vice Rector of Krosno State College, which was established as recently as 1999, on the site of my father and uncle's grade school just a stone's throw from their former family home.

Stephen and Wladek arranged for Sol to give a lecture to the American students in Kraków and to the general public at Krosno State College, where he spoke in Polish. The American students to whom Sol spoke were especially moved, and a few of them were in tears and came up to him after his talk and gave him a hug. One student told Sol that listening to him had been the most important educational experience of her life. Sol and Jack also received a special guided tour of Auschwitz; and while they were inside one of the barracks exhibits, some Orthodox Jews overheard Sol talking to the guide and asked him to speak impromptu to the students who were with them. Jack said it was amazing to watch them gather around his father, completely surrounding him, wanting "him to speak about his personal experience. ... Here was a *real* survivor, someone who had experienced the Holocaust first-hand." Sol felt like a VIP, and he enjoyed this immensely. Like my father, he was able to bracket the moving experiences of grief from the uplifting moments of his trip.

As for me, I am a child of a survivor and still wonder what it means for my family's legacy. In 2009 I gave a keynote lecture about my family's story at the Legacy of the Holocaust conference in Kraków, and like my uncle, I spoke at Krosno State College as well. The director of a Holocaust studies program in Israel who attended the conference told me that as a child of a survivor I am, in psychotherapist Dina Wardi's words, a "memorial candle," a reminder of a horrific past that we all hope will never be forgotten.[8] Then, she added, "You have status." I know what this means but I do not know what this means. It is my sense that in the absence of the actual survivors, those of us who have lived with them, who have known them intimately, give others some sense of authentic connection to the past. As Menachem Rosensaft, a founding member of the International Network of Children of Jewish Holocaust Survivors, suggests, "We are, I believe, unique in that, while we did not experience the Holocaust, we have a closer personal link to it than anyone other than our parents."[9]

But what, at its heart, is this desire to connect to this horrific past? Why do people want to experience the victims' anguish? Are they looking for some meaning for their own suffering, or seeking a lesson for the future? For Jews, as historian Peter Novick observes, perhaps it is a way of feeling solidarity with their ethnic kin, united in the common "knowledge that but for the immigration of near or distant ancestors, they would have shared the fate of European Jewry."[10] For non-Jews, it may be a way to say, to themselves and others, "I am not like those who did this to you." Hopefully, it will be a reminder to all of us that what happened during the Holocaust should happen "Never again"—to Jews or anyone else[11]—and that none of us should ever have to repeat my grandfather's parting words: "Children, save yourselves!"

The Berger family (1964). Above (left to right): Michael, Jack Weissbluth, Sol. Below (left to right): Rose, Eleanor, Mildred, Frances, Gertrude.

Michael at gate of Auschwitz I (1989).

Michael at
Auschwitz I (1989).

Sol with Henryk Duchowski (2008).

Children, Save Yourselves!

Memorial stone at mass grave site near Barwinek (1989).

Appendix

LETTERS TO MY FATHER AND UNCLE

The following are excerpts from student letters and thank you notes written to my father, Michael Berger, and my uncle, Sol Berger, after they spoke about their experiences to various classes. The letters to Michael, written in the early 1990s, are from high-school students in the Los Angeles area and college students at the University of Wisconsin-Whitewater. The letters to Sol, written in 2013, are from high-school students in the Los Angeles area.

Letters to Michael

I learned from you what a textbook cannot teach.

You really changed the way I saw the Holocaust. I've seen all the movies, and teachers have told me the facts. But to actually hear someone who was really there ... hit me like a brick.

Your visit to our class was a gift that I will treasure always.

I am glad that you are able to tell your story, for it will have an impact on me for a long time to come.

You really opened my eyes. ... I feel honored to have met and been able to listen to someone like you.

I will never forget your story and will always keep it in my heart.

I know I shall never get a chance like this again to meet a person such as yourself.

Children, Save Yourselves!

I want to thank you so very much for coming into our class and reliving your painful past to help us learn better. It takes an incredible amount of courage to do such a thing.

I envy your courage for the time you've gone through the Holocaust and for telling us about it. I promise to tell my children and my children's children that the Holocaust did happen.

I've been studying [the Holocaust] since the eighth grade, but I must say your speech moved me emotionally. I've heard speeches from many Holocaust survivors, but yours was different. It gave me courage and hope, and I thank you dearly for that.

I admire and respect you tremendously for your strength, intellect, honor, and all of the other attributes that have brought you to where you are today.

I will remember you always. You taught me so much about human nature and willpower. I hope I will be as successful in teaching my students.

Now I know what I want to do for the rest of my life. I want to help people and educate them about ignorance so nothing like this would ever happen again.

As we were studying the Holocaust before you came, I felt for the Jews and others who had experienced it. But I wasn't moved by it until I sat directly in front of you and listened with my heart and mind. ... I am so sorry that you had to go through what you did, but I am very thankful that you are alive and healthy today to share your experiences with us. I will tell it to my kids and share with them everything that I've learned from you!

The experiences you shared with us have made me realize how lucky we really are in the U.S. ... It has made me value my freedom and liberty, which sometimes we take for granted.

Even though most of the survivors will [eventually] be gone, ... I want you to know that my children and grandchildren will be taught about the Holocaust.

I kept thinking, "This man actually lived through the Holocaust and was actually there." ... I will never forget your ... story.

Letters to Sol

Thank you for a life changing opportunity to hear your story.

Your story really touched me deeply.

Thank you ... for your courage to tell your inspirational story.

Your story of perseverance was so inspiring.

You are a very strong and courageous man. I admire you and thank you for sharing your story with us.

God bless your life. You have very much inspired me to ... appreciate my life ... [and] work harder to accomplish my goals.

Through your words you helped me realize that we are blessed to be U.S. citizens and that we should take advantage of the many opportunities we have here.

You are truly an inspiration. Hearing your story has made me see that even though we get caught in difficult situations, we can endure and come out strong. Like you, I hope for a world where people are good to one another and that this kind of hatred never happens again. Through reaching our hearts, you are making this a reality.

Children, Save Yourselves!

Notes

PROLOGUE

1. Sources for this Prologue include Ronald J. Berger, *The Holocaust, Religion, and the Politics of Collective Memory: Beyond Sociology* (New Brunswick, NJ: Transaction, 2013); Ronald J. Berger, *Surviving the Holocaust: A Life Course Perspective* (New York: Routledge, 2011); Helen Epstein, *Children of the Holocaust: Conversations with Sons and Daughters of Survivors* (New York: Penguin, 1979); Peter Novick, *The Holocaust in American Life* (Boston: Houghton Mifflin, 1999); and Arlene Stein, *Reluctant Witnesses: Survivors, Their Children, and the Rise of Holocaust Consciousness* (New York: Oxford University Press, 2014).

2. The Holocaust took the lives of some six million Jews. This amounted to about 60 percent of European Jewry and a third of the world's Jewish population. To be sure, all too many other groups suffered at the hands of the Nazis as well. When one adds the murder of Gypsies, Poles, Slavs, Soviet civilians and prisoners of war, gay men, the disabled and mentally ill, among others—the number of innocent dead is far greater. At the same time, no other group was as disproportionately affected or targeted for total annihilation as the Jews.

3. My books include *Constructing a Collective Memory of the Holocaust: A Life History of Two Brothers' Survival* (Boulder: University Press of Colorado, 1995); *Fathoming the Holocaust: A Social Problems Approach* (New York: Aldine de Gruyter, 2003); *The Holocaust, Religion, and the Politics of Collective Memory*; and *Surviving the Holocaust*.

4. The documentary was produced by David Notowitz for Rhino Records in Los Angeles.

5. Alexander Bialywos White, *Be a Mensch: A Legacy of the Holocaust* (Scottsdale, AZ: self-published memoir, 2004).

6. Gusta and Solomon Berger, *Love, Survival, and the American Dream* (Marina del Rey, CA: jMo5000, 2013).

7. I am a trained researcher, and when first documenting my father's and uncle's story, I made every effort to ascertain as much as possible whether the factual components of their accounts such as dates

of particular events, travel distances, and the like were accurate. This involved consulting other published sources that are relevant to their experiences. I also interviewed a non-Jewish Polish couple from their hometown, Taduesz and Maria Duchowski, who corroborated elements of my father's and uncle's account and contributed details they had neglected to mention. Their part in the story will be told later in the book.

It is nonetheless true that our recollections of the past may become distorted over time. Traumatic events like the Holocaust are more likely to be remembered in vivid detail, but it is not uncommon for people to remember the past somewhat differently as time goes by. When Sol told his story to his grandson Jesse in the last years of his life, his memory of a few details differed from what both he (and my father) had told me earlier. In these instances, I am inclined to accept the earlier version of the story as more likely to be accurate.

1. KROSNO

1. Sources on Poland for this chapter include Rita Steinhardt Botwinick, *A History of the Holocaust: From Ideology to Annihilation* (Upper Saddle River, NJ: Prentice-Hall, 2001); Sophie Caplan, "Polish and German Anti-Semitism," in *Why Germany? National Socialist Anti-Semitism in European Context*, ed. John Milfull (Oxford: Berg, 1993); Israel Gutman (ed.), *Encyclopedia of the Holocaust* (New York: Macmillan, 1990); Celia Heller, *On the Edge of Destruction: Jews of Poland Between the Two World Wars* (New York: Columbia University Press, 1977); Aleksander Hertz, *The Jews in Polish Culture* (Evanston, IL: Northwestern University Press, 1988); and Nechama Tec, *When Light Pierced the Darkness: Christian Rescue of Jews in Nazi-Occupied Poland* (New York: Oxford University Press, 1986).

2. During the German occupation of World War II, Ukrainians were particularly likely to collaborate with the Nazis.

3. Gutman, *Encyclopedia of the Holocaust*, p. 1153.

4. Besides my own family's testimony, other sources on Krosno include Joram Kagan, *Poland's Jewish Heritage* (New York: Hippocrene, 1992); White, *Be a Mensch*; and information that is available on the website of *JewishGen KehilaLinks* (www.kehilalinks.jewishgen.org).

5. For the purpose of this book, I have used the English translations of the Polish names, which are the names my father and uncle generally used to describe their family. One exception is that they more often referred to their brother Moses by his Hebrew name Moishe. In Joshua's case, his Polish given name was Osias, which best translates to Oscar in English; it also translates in Hebrew as Joshua.

6. When World War I broke out and Russian Cossacks invaded Polish territory, Jacob was recruited into the Austrian Army because Galacia was part of Austria at that time. The rest of the family took refuge in Budapest, Hungary, where Joshua was born. The family returned to Krosno after the war.

7. On the term Goldene Medina, which is a Yiddish phrase, see Deborah Dash Moore, *To the Golden Cities: Pursuing the American Jewish Dream in Miami and L.A.* (Cambridge, MA: Harvard University Press, 1994).

8. During Kristallnacht, which is translated as Crystal Night or Night of the Broken Glass, Jewish businesses and synagogues were attacked by Nazi troops; and about a hundred Jews were killed, countless injured, and some 30,000 arrested and sent to concentration camps.

9. Samuel P. Oliner and Pearl M. Oliner, *The Altruistic Personality: Rescuers of Jews in Nazi Europe* (New York: Free Press, 1988). Tec, *When Light Pierced the Darkness*.

10. As grown men, both brothers stood about 5 feet, 4 inches tall.

11. Menachem Begin was the Polish leader of Betar. Upon his arrival to Palestine, he became a commander of the Irgun, a paramilitary organization that drew most of its members from Betar. Begin later served as prime minister of Israel from 1977-1983.

2. THE INVASION

1. Yiddish is a centuries-old European dialect that combines German and Hebrew and provides a cultural link between Jews from different communities, regions, and nations.

2. It is possible that if Michael, Sol, and Joshua hadn't left Soviet-occupied Poland to return home, they could have been caught up in the mass killing of Jews that accompanied the Nazi invasion of Soviet territory in June 1941.

3. THE OCCUPATION

1. To be sure, the Nazis were no friends of the Poles. The political, intellectual, and religious leadership of Poland was decimated, and some three million Gentiles were killed. See Richard Lukas, *Forgotten Holocaust: The Poles Under German Occupation 1939-1944* (New York: Hippocrene, 1986).

4. CHILDREN, SAVE YOURSELVES!

1. In May, prior to the invasion, Sol witnessed Hitler, Mussolini, and Hungarian Prime Minister László Bárdossy pass through Krosno in black Mercedes convertibles. He was standing about 20 meters away.

2. In July 1941, Reinhard Heydrich, a high-ranking Nazi official, presented Hermann Göring, Hitler's second-in-command, with a written order he had prepared for Göring's signature. The order authorized Heydrich to make "all necessary preparations with regard to organizational, practical and financial aspects for an overall solution of the Jewish question in the German sphere of influence in Europe" and to submit "to me promptly an overall plan of the preliminary ... measures for the execution of the intended final solution."

By fall the outlines of the plan began to emerge. Experimental gassing of Jews at Auschwitz was undertaken, and construction of death camps at Bełżec and Chełmno began. In January 1942 Heydrich convened the Wannsee Conference, at which time the decision to proceed with the Final Solution was officially transmitted to a group of high-ranking Nazi functionaries. See Christopher R. Browning, *The Origins of the Final Solution: The Evolution of Nazi Jewish Policy September 1939-March 1942* (London: William Heinemann, 2004).

3. The SS began as Hitler's defense corps and expanded to include surveillance and intelligence operations, mobile military units that killed civilians, and operation of the concentration camp system. See Omar Bartov, *Hitler's Army: Soldiers, Nazis, and War in the Third Reich* (New York: Oxford University Press, 1992); and Richard Rhodes, *Masters of Death: The SS-Einsatzgrupen and the Invention of the Holocaust* (New York: Knopf, 2002).

4. White, *Be a Mensch*.

5. Organisation Todt was named after its founder, engineer Dr. Fritz Todt.

6. Alex White recalled that the rows were five across.

7. Martin Gilbert, *Routledge Atlas of the Holocaust*, 4th ed. (New York: Routledge, 2009).

8. In his initial account of this episode that I recorded in the early 1990s, Sol recalled staying one night at the home of the Pole who was managing the tailor shop. In that account he included details of a conversation he had with this Pole. See Berger, *Constructing a Collective Memory of the Holocaust* and *Surviving the Holocaust*.

5. PASSING

1. Oliner and Oliner, *The Altruistic Personality*. Tec, *When Light Pierced the Darkness*.

2. Russian partisan groups were located further to the east.

3. Gutman, *Encyclopedia of the Holocaust*.

4. Hungary was an ally of Germany during the war, and the government was complicit in the deportation of Hungarian Jews to the death camps.

6. THE CAMPS

1. Sources on the concentration camps for this chapter include Debórah Dwork and Robert Jan van Pelt, *Auschwitz: 1270 to the Present* (New York: W. W. Norton, 2002); Gutman, *Encyclopedia of the Holocaust*; Walter Laqueur (ed.), *The Holocaust Encyclopedia* (New Haven, CT: Yale University Press, 2001); and Sybille Steinbacher, *Auschwitz: A History* (New York: Penguin, 2005).

2. Although Michael thought that Moses was shot outside of Szebnie, after the war a survivor told Sol that he had seen Moses hanging from a rope behind a barracks in Auschwitz. We do not know for sure what happened.

3. Overall, 5 to 10 percent of prisoners taken to concentration camps by rail died en route. See Claude Lanzmann, *Shoah: An Oral History of the Holocaust* (New York: Pantheon, 1985).

4. Other survivor accounts I have read and heard about indicate that the prisoners were ordered to line up in rows of five. This discrepancy from Michael's account may be due to the fact that these individuals arrived at a later date.

5. Mengele is one of the most notorious Nazi doctors, known particularly for his horrific experiments on some 1,500 sets of twin children—subjecting them to X-rays and various chemicals, ultimately killing them so he could examine their internal organs—aimed at learning about the causes of twin births. See Robert Jay Lifton, *The Nazi Doctors: Medical Killing and the Psychology of Genocide* (New York: Basic Books, 1986).

6. The warehouses were termed Kanada because Canada was a symbol of wealth to the prisoners.

7. AUSCHWITZ-MONOWITZ

1. Two of the most well-known survivor accounts, Primo Levi's *Survival in Auschwitz* (New York: Collier, 1960), and Elie Wiesel's *Night* (New York: Hill and Wang, 1960), were written by Monowitz survivors. While Michael arrived in Monowitz in December 1943, Levi arrived in late January 1944, and Wiesel in May 1944.

2. Actual production of Buna never got underway because of Allied air attacks on the facility, and only small quantities of synthetic fuel were made. For an in-depth account of the I.G. Farben corporation, see Peter Hayes, *Industry and Ideology: IG Farben in the Nazi Era* (Cambridge, UK: Cambridge University Press, 1987).

3. The term Muselmänn (singular) or Muselmänner (plural) apparently derived from the German word for Muslim and was based on the fallacious belief that Muslims were fatalistic and indifferent to their environment

4. In the late 1990s, after my father had passed away, Herman's son located me through an internet search and told me his father was living in Canada. I had the opportunity to talk with Herman by phone, and he expressed his deep gratitude toward my father for helping him get through his camp experience, including sharing provisions with him. According to Herman's son, Herman was reluctant to talk about his experiences, in large part, he thought, because of the sexual abuse he experienced in the camps.

5. After the war, Michael met this man in Munich, who seemed pleased to see Michael alive. Michael did not feel the same about him.

6. Levi, *Survival in Auschwitz*, p. 68.

7. Holocaust scholar Lawrence Langer makes a distinction between acts that are "selfish" and acts that are "self-ish." "The selfish act ignores

the needs of others through choice when the agent is in a position to help without injuring one's self in any appreciable way. Selfishness is motivated by greed, indifference, [and] malice. ... The self-ish act [is one in which the agent] is vividly aware of the needs of others but because of the nature of the situation is unable to choose freely the generous impulse that a more compassionate nature yearns to express" (*Holocaust Testimonies: The Ruins of Memory* [New Haven, CT: Yale University Press, 1991], p. 124).

8. For accounts of resistance activities in the camps, see Yitzhak Arad, *Operation Reinhard Death Camps: Belzec, Sobibor, Treblinka* (Bloomington: Indiana University Press, 1987); Laqueur, *The Holocaust Encyclopedia*; Thomas Maher, "Threat, Resistance, and Collective Action: The Cases of Sobibór, Treblinka, and Auschwitz," *American Sociological Review*, vol. 25 (2010, pp. 252-72); and Filip Müller, *Eyewitness Auschwitz: Three Years in the Gas Chambers* (New York: Stein and Day, 1979).

8. THE DEATH MARCH

1. Primo Levi was one of the survivors who stayed behind. See also Gutman, *Encyclopedia of the Holocaust*; and Laqueur, *The Holocaust Encyclopedia*.

2. See Elie Wiesel's *Night* for his account of the Death March.

3. See Chapter 7, note 4.

4. Fred eventually immigrated to Chicago.

5. The U.S. captain was one of about 550,000 Jewish men and women who served in the U.S. Armed Forces during the war, a level of participation that caused Jews in the United States to more fully identify themselves as full-blooded Americans, rather than as an ethnic minority per se (Moore, *To the Golden Cities*). Jewish Americans were proud of their service, and European Jews were proud of them too. Michael was elated to see that a Jew could exercise such power over the Germans. He had always thought that Jews were better off in the United States than in other countries, and the fact that a Jew could be a captain in the U.S. Army only reinforced this belief. In the Polish Army, Jews had not been considered capable of being good soldiers and were not allowed to rise to a rank higher than sergeant, unless they were trained as a medical doctor. This ate away at their self-confidence and made them feel inferior. But now they felt pride to know that Jews had contributed to the Allied war effort.

9. GUSTA

1. The state of Israel was not established until 1948. Before then, Palestine remained a territory of Great Britain, which was resolutely opposed to relinquishing control. But Jewish armed resistance and changing international opinion eventually led Britain to acquiesce, and in October 1947 the newly established United Nations passed a resolution to establish a Jewish state. See Yehuda Bauer, *Flight and Rescue* (New York: Random House, 1970); Yehuda Bauer, *Rethinking the Holocaust* (New Haven CT: Yale University Press, 2001); and Martin Gilbert, *Israel: A History* (New York: William Morrow, 1998).

2. Gusta was never reunited with her parents or other siblings.

3. Gusta eventually learned that her sister Mina had survived. Unlike Gusta, Mina had been allowed to cross the border into Germany. She worked on a farm for a German family, all the while passing as a Catholic Pole. Mina eventually settled in New York. Although Mina and Gusta heard reports from witnesses who said they had seen their brother Ben and sister Dora after the war, neither of them ever heard from them again.

4. Sol was given the name Shlomo Harari (Harari means Berger in Greek).

5. Of her feelings at the time, Gusta said, "Was I in love? I don't know. I was young and alone. Maybe God was telling me to stay under the tree. Maybe I did not know what else to do, except finally say yes. The only thing I knew was that I trusted Sol to take care of me."

6. Belgrade is currently the capital of Serbia.

7. Zagreb is currently the capital of Croatia.

8. The Jewish Brigade, which was formed in late 1945 and fought the Germans in Italy, was composed of Palestinian Jews commanded by British-Jewish officers.

9. Michael Brenner, "Displaced Persons," in *The Holocaust Encyclopaedia* (ed. Laqueur). Hagit Lavsky, "Displaced Persons, Jewish," in *Encyclopedia of the Holocaust* (ed. Gutman).

10. Representatives from the Jewish paramilitary group Haganah were in charge of the illegal immigration operation, which was being suppressed by the British.

10. LIVING IN LIMBO

1. Lavsky, "Displaced Persons, Jewish," p. 378. Michael and Sol were among about 200,000 European Jews living in displaced person camps in May 1945. See also Bauer, *Rethinking the Holocaust*; and Brenner, "Displaced Persons."

2. At this time only families with children were allowed to buy eggs.

3. During her time in London, Gusta was reunited with her sister Mina for the first time (see Chapter 9, note 3). In October 1949, Gusta, Jackie, Toni, and Leo took a plane to Frankfurt, Germany, to see her. Gusta recalled, "It was beyond good to see Mina and hear her voice again. I knew now that if anything happened to me, Jackie would have someone from my family to look after him. My prayers had been answered."

11. THE GOLDENE MEDINA

1. For research on prewar and wartime U.S. immigration policy and efforts (or lack thereof) to help the Jews, see Richard Breitman and Alan M. Kraut, *American Refugee Policy and European Jewry, 1933-1945* (Bloomington: Indiana University Press, 1987); Robert N. Rosen, *Saving the Jews: Franklin D. Roosevelt and the Holocaust* (New York: Thunder's Mouth Press, 2006); William D. Rubenstein, *The Myth of Rescue: Why the Democracies Could Not Have Saved More Jews* (New York: Routledge, 1997); and David S. Wyman, *The Abandonment of the Jews: America and the Holocaust, 1941-1945* (New York: Pantheon, 1984).

2. Leonard Dinnerstein, *America and the Survivors of the Holocaust* (New York: Columbia University Press, 1982). William Helmreich, *Against All Odds: Holocaust Survivors and the Successful Lives They Made in America* (New York: Simon and Schuster, 1992). Howard M. Sachar, *A History of the Jews in America* (New York: Vintage, 1992).

3. Jeffrey C. Alexander, *The Civil Sphere* (New York: Oxford University Press, 2006, p. 482).

4. Paul's European name was Isaackowitz. Mildred (1923-2007), my mother, was born in Peekskill, New York, and moved with her family to Glendale, California, when she was a young girl. Her mother, Fanny Isaackowitz (1895-1975), had emigrated from Hungary, and her father, Samuel Klempner (1889-1960), from the ambiguous border region of Poland and Russia, before World War II.

5. Sources on Los Angeles Jews for this chapter include Hasia R. Diner, *The Jews of the United States* (Berkeley: University of California Press, 2004); Moore, *To the Golden Cities*; and Edward S. Shapiro, *A Time for Healing: American Jewry since World War II* (Baltimore: Johns Hopkins University Press, 1992).

6. Diner, *The Jews of the United States*. Seymour Martin Lipset and Earl Raab, *Jews and the New American Scene* (Cambridge, MA: Harvard University Press, 1995). Moore, *To the Golden Cities*.

7. Richard Alba and Victor Nee, *Remaking the American Mainstream: Assimilation and Contemporary Immigration* (Cambridge, MA: Harvard University Press, 2003). Ivan Light and Steven J. Gold, *Ethnic Economies* (San Diego, CA: Academic Press, 2000).

8. The historical relationship between Jewish merchants and African-American residents has been fraught with controversy, as some blacks have regarded Jews as interlopers in their communities. For discussion of the tensions between African Americans and Jewish Americans, see Paul Berman (ed.), *Blacks and Jews: Alliances and Arguments* (New York: Delta, 1994); Diner, *The Jews of the United States*; Eric Goldstein, *The Price of Whiteness: Jews, Race, and American Identity* (Princeton, NJ: Princeton University Press, 2006); Moore, *To the Golden Cities*; Novick, *The Holocaust in American Life*; and Shapiro, *A Time for Healing*.

9. Helmreich, *Against All Odds*, p. 117.

10. Alexander, *The Civil Sphere*, p. 523. The idea of a common Judeo-Christian tradition was initially propagated by Jews and Jewish sympathizers in response to wartime rhetoric that characterized the major thrust of Nazism as an assault on "Christian civilization" (Novick, *The Holocaust in American Life*). It gained popular currency through Will Herberg's best-selling *Protestant-Catholic-Jew: A Study in Religious Sociology* (Garden City, NY: Doubleday), which was published in 1955. Herberg argued that Americans had adopted a tripartite religious scheme that expressed a common inheritance of moral and spiritual values. During the Cold War with the Soviet Union, this view served to unify Americans vis-à-vis atheistic communism (Shapiro, *A Time for Healing*).

11. Herbert Gans, "Symbolic Ethnicity: The Future of Ethnic Groups and Cultures in America," *Ethnic and Racial Studies*, vol. 2 (1979, pp. 1-20). See also Karen Brodkin, *How Jews Became White Folks and What That Says about Race in America* (New Brunswick, NJ: Rutgers University Press, 1998).

Children, Save Yourselves!

12. Samuel Freedman, *Jew vs. Jew: The Struggle for the Soul of American Jewry* (New York: Simon and Schuster, 2000, p. 339).

13. Lipset and Raab, *Jews and the New American Scene*, p. 46.

EPILOGUE

1. Helmreich, *Against All Odds*, p. 83.

2. Psychiatrists Leo Eitinger and William Niederland are noteworthy for their clinical work in developing the "survivor syndrome" construct, which assumes that survivors suffered from problems such as persistent anxiety, depression, and emotional numbness. See Leo Eitinger, *Concentration Camp Survivors in Norway and Israel* (London: Allen and Unwin, 1964); and William C. Niederland, "Psychiatric Disorders Among Persecution Victims: A Contribution to the Understanding of Concentration Camp Pathology and Its After-Effects," *Journal of Nervous and Mental Diseases*, vol. 139 (1964, pp. 458-474).

3. Shamai Davidson, *Holding on to Humanity – the Message of Holocaust Survivors: The Shamai Davidson Papers*, ed. Israel W. Charny (New York: New York University Press, 1992). Zev Harel, Boaz Kahana, and Eva Kahana, "Psychological Well-Being Among Holocaust Survivors and Immigrants in Israel," *Journal of Traumatic Stress*, vol. 1 (1988, pp. 413-429). Aaron Hass, *The Aftermath: Living with the Holocaust* (Cambridge, UK: Cambridge University Press, 1995). Boaz Kahana, Zev Harel, and Eva Kahana, "Predictors of Psychological Well-Being Among Survivors of the Holocaust," in *Human Adaptation to Extreme Stress*, eds. John Preston Wilson et al. (New York: Plenum, 1988). G. R. Leon et al., "Survivors of the Holocaust and Their Children: Current Status and Adjustment," *Journal of Personality and Social Psychology*, vol. 41 (1981, pp. 503-516). Paul Matussek, *Internment in Concentration Camps and Its Consequences* (New York: Springer-Verlag, 1975). Peter Suedfeld, *Life After the Ashes: The Postwar Pain, and Resilience, of Young Holocaust Survivors* (Washington, DC: U.S. Holocaust Memorial Museum Center for Advanced Holocaust Studies, 2002).

Psychiatric researchers also have assumed that symptoms of psychopathology would inevitably be transmitted to children. But according to psychologist Aaron Hass, "Children of survivors are extremely diverse in their personality profiles, their levels of achievement, and their lifestyles.

Previous generalizations have often been founded on a blatant disregard for the rules of scientific inquiry" (*In the Shadow of the Holocaust: The Second Generation* [New York: Cornell University Press, 1990, pp. 35-36]). Indeed, studies that compare non-clinical populations of second-generation children with the general population find little difference in symptoms of psychopathology. See Natan Kellermann, "Psychopathology in Children of Holocaust Survivors: A Review of the Research Literature," *Israel Journal of Psychiatry and Related Sciences*, vol. 38 (2001, pp. 36-46); and Fran Klein-Parker, "Dominant Attitudes of Adult Children of Holocaust Survivors toward Their Parents," in *Human Adaptation to Extreme Stress*, eds. John Preston et al. (New York: Plenum, 1988).

4. Davidson, *Holding on to Humanity*, p. 22.

5. For a while, after my father retired from the liquor business and was acclimating himself to his new routines, he did experience depression. But this was in large part due to physical health problems, which were subsequently rectified through surgery, upon which his psychological health improved. My uncle, too, suffered from depression when he retired from the liquor business. He sought out counseling and renewed his zest for life. He became an active member of various community groups and served as president of his congregation as well as the Beverly Hills chapter of B'nai B'rith.

6. Kahana et al, "Predictors of Psychological Well-Being," p. 189.

7. Taduesz Duchowski and his son Henryk were the ones who located this grave, which is in a forest about 30 kilometers from Krosno. Alex White, a survivor of Krosno, is skeptical that the elderly Jews who were taken away on August 10, 1942, are actually buried there along with Jews from nearby towns who also were killed around that time. We do not really know for sure, but it is the only grave marker we have for our European family.

8. Dina Wari, *Memorial Candles: Children of the Holocaust* (London: Tavistock, 1992).

9. Quoted in Ellen Fine, "The Absent Memory," in *Writing and Rewriting the Holocaust*, ed. Berel Lang (New York: Holmes and Meier, 1988). See also Gary Weissman, *Fantasies of Witnessing: Postwar Efforts to Experience the Holocaust* (Ithaca, NY: Cornell University Press, 2004).

10. Novick, *The Holocaust in American Life*, p. 190.

Children, Save Yourselves!

11. Regretfully, it has happened and will likely happen again, because humanity has not really learned the lesson of the Holocaust. Among the most well-known post-World War II genocides are the ones that took place in Cambodia in the 1970s, Bosnia and Rwanda in the 1990s, and Darfur in the 2000s. See Daniel Jonah Goldhagen, *Worse Than War: Genocide, Eliminationism, and the Ongoing Assault on Humanity* (New York: Public Affairs, 2009); and Samantha Power, *"A Problem from Hell": America and the Age of Genocide* (New York: Basic Books, 2002).

About the Author

Ronald J. Berger is professor emeritus of sociology at the University of Wisconsin-Whitewater. He has published numerous books and articles on topics that include crime and criminal justice, disability, and the Holocaust. Born and raised in Los Angeles, California, he currently lives in McFarland, Wisconsin.